TEACHING
EMPATHY

TEACHING EMPATHY

Strategies for Building Emotional
Intelligence in Today's Students

Suzanna E. Henshon, Ph.D.

PRUFROCK PRESS INC.
WACO, TEXAS

Library of Congress Control Number:2019944689

Copyright ©2019, Prufrock Press Inc.

Edited by Stephanie McCauley

Cover and layout design by Micah Benson

ISBN-13: 978-1-61821-905-3

Printed in the United States of America.

At the time of this book's publication, all facts and figures cited are the most current available. All telephone numbers, addresses, and website URLs are accurate and active. All publications, organizations, websites, and other resources exist as described in the book, and all have been verified. The authors and Prufrock Press Inc. make no warranty or guarantee concerning the information and materials given out by organizations or content found at websites, and we are not responsible for any changes that occur after this book's publication. If you find an error, please contact Prufrock Press Inc.

Prufrock Press Inc.
P.O. Box 8813
Waco, TX 76714-8813
Phone: (800) 998-2208
Fax: (800) 240-0333
http://www.prufrock.com

Dedication

This book is dedicated to my mother, Elaine Henshon, whose life was filled with love and compassion. With joy in every footstep, Elaine guided her friends and family into a world filled with starlight and endless rainbows. She read early drafts of this book and provided invaluable advice and encouragement.

Table of Contents

Acknowledgments. 1

Introduction:
Why Empathy?. 3

Chapter 1:
What Is Empathy? 11

Chapter 2:
How Can You Create an Empathetic Classroom? 37

Chapter 3:
How Can You Teach Empathy?. 59

Chapter 4:
How Does Emotional Intelligence Relate to Empathy? . . 73

Chapter 5:
How Can You Maintain Empathy in Your Classroom? . . 83

Chapter 6:
How Can Students Give Back to Society?. 99

Chapter 7:
How Can You Use Technology to Promote Empathy? . . 115

Chapter 8:
How Can You Lead a Schoolwide Empathy Initiative? . . 125

Conclusion:
What Is Your Future Vision of Empathy? 137

References 145

About the Author 151

Acknowledgments

I would like to thank Stephanie McCauley, Joel McIntosh, and the entire staff at Prufrock Press for supporting this project. Stephanie McCauley made excellent suggestions and recommendations that improved the overall quality of this text in countless ways. I couldn't ask for a better editor.

I would like to acknowledge the teachers who have inspired me over the years. In particular, I would like to thank Dr. Joyce VanTassel-Baska, Dr. Dominic Failla, Dr. Don Ambrose, Dr. David Leslie, Dr. Norma Day-Vines, Professor Nancy Schoenberger, Lori Cornelius, Emily Vallier, and Chuck Vernon. I would also like to thank my students for their input on this project.

I would like to thank my family, including my parents, Elaine and Thomas Henshon. Lastly, I would like to express gratitude to Matthew, Andrew, Brian, David, Meghan, Amanda, William, Mark, James, Cecily, Molly, Owen, Maeve, and Sarah Henshon for their encouragement.

Why Empathy?

When you start to develop your powers of empathy
and imagination, the whole world opens up for you.
—Susan Sarandon

Why did you become a teacher? Did you hope to make a difference in the world by sharing your knowledge with young people?
What could be more important? Empathy is the most important way
that people can connect with each other. Every student needs to experience empathy in his or her life. Teaching facts and figures is not
enough; empathy is the first step toward creating a caring school and
a compassionate world.

Can one person make an impact? Yes, you can make a difference
in a child's world. You can be the teacher who inspires students forever. You can be the educator who brings positive change to your
school. The work is challenging, but you're ready. You *can* do this.
This book will help you teach empathy in your classroom. Students of
all ability levels can learn empathy. It doesn't matter whether you're
working with general education, special education, or gifted learners.
This book is for you.

It's vital that we teach empathy in today's classrooms. One of the reasons for this is to combat bullying. According to a teaching module from the American Psychological Association (Graham, n.d.), between 40%–80% of students experience bullying at school at some point. Although many districts have implemented antibullying programs, there's still work to be done. Bullying goes on 24 hours a day, 7 days a week, through cyberbullying and other methods.

More kids seem to be bullied today than ever before. A&E's documentary series *Undercover High School* profiles young adults who return to high school in their mid-20s, only to discover that bullying is worse than ever. This is only one of many shows and series that document this behavior in today's schools. We must teach students why it is important to treat each other well rather than simply punishing bullying behaviors. This book will also dive into many other benefits of teaching and learning empathy.

CRITICAL QUESTIONS

The following are some important questions about empathy that we will discuss throughout the chapters.

What Is Empathy?

Empathy is the ability to connect with other people and to understand their thoughts and feelings. Empathy is considering another person's experience and seeing the world from another perspective. Empathy exists along a continuum, and the best way to measure empathy is in a situational context.

Empathy overlaps with other skills that educators are trying to instill in students, including emotional intelligence, interpersonal intelligence, and intrapersonal intelligence. As educators working in diverse classrooms, we must teach our students to be caring people, not just to care about grades. Empathy is a very important educational initiative, not just a soft skill. In fact, empathy is crucial for developing strong leaders (Bell, 2009; Deobald, 2019). Empathy is making a huge impact across many disciplines. Why shouldn't empathy make an impact in your classroom, too?

How Can You Create an Empathetic Classroom?

You can teach with empathy and show concern toward your students. As an educator, you can develop a caring classroom by taking several steps to introduce and maintain empathy.

Empathy cannot be a top-down movement; it must come directly from students. Empathy must be a way of life, not just a vocabulary word that we teach students during a lesson plan. We must live and breathe empathy for this movement to work.

How Can You Teach Empathy?

In an ideal world, all students would enter school with the ability to show concern toward each other. Unfortunately, we don't live in a perfect world. Students come to our schools with diverse backgrounds, and empathy isn't modeled in every home. So we must grow empathy in our classrooms. Students may never have the chance to experience this concept otherwise.

Students have different levels of empathy extending along a continuum. By the time children are 5 years old, these differences become apparent in educational settings. Some students live in homes without books, while other children live in houses without empathy. As educators, we can teach empathy through a variety of methods—from instructional to situational. Teaching empathy is a holistic process, merging naturally with the curriculum.

How Does Emotional Intelligence Relate to Empathy?

Emotional intelligence is the ability to connect with your own feelings and to understand what other people are going through. Empathy is a facet of emotional intelligence. If you can imagine yourself in someone else's situation, your emotional intelligence capacity will rise. Empathy is intricately linked to emotional intelligence, and these two qualities can be developed concurrently.

How Can You Maintain Empathy in Your Classroom?

Students will learn the importance of empathy by watching how you act in different situations. When you bring caring qualities into your life, you set a wonderful example for your class. Don't sweat the small things; think about the big picture. Becoming a caring person is a lifelong process. When students are treated with empathy, they share their gifts with the world. Empathy can begin in your classroom and grow into a huge movement within your school and community.

Your students can pursue empathy at the highest level. To get this movement started, you will create a caring classroom in which empathy is valued and nurtured. Many of your colleagues are trying to do the same thing. Why not work together to create a caring school?

How Can Students Give Back to Society?

Your students have qualities and personal resources that can never be measured on a test. Often students feel like they aren't prepared to give back to society. That's where you come in—to give your students the boost of confidence they need to begin giving back to a world that has given them so much.

How Can We Promote Empathy Through Media and Technology?

Media and technology can be used to bring students together in positive ways. When students use technology positively, they create a cohesive academic environment. With media and technology, you can create a caring school in which everyone feels valued.

How Can You Lead a Schoolwide Empathy Initiative?

As a teacher, you lead your students through knowledge and information. But can you lead your students toward empathy? Can you make the extra effort to develop your leadership abilities in this area?

Empathy requires the support of administrators, staff, teachers, parents, and students. With the support of these stakeholders, empathy will become a natural part of your school's atmosphere. Why not start an empathy building team today? It sounds challenging, but nothing is more rewarding than sharing your gift of leadership in new and dynamic ways. You can lead your students and colleagues to lives filled with empathy.

What Is Your Future Vision of Empathy?

You can't predict tomorrow's events, but you can plan for a brighter future. You can build the foundation for a caring school and world. But all of your planning will have minimal results without the support of your students.

The future of empathy lies in your students. With your support, students will take the first steps toward developing empathy. Even if children haven't experienced empathy at home, you can inspire them toward empathy. As Dr. Seuss once said, "To the world you may be one person, but to one person you may be the world."

HOW TO USE THIS BOOK

In Chapter 1, we'll study a general definition of empathy. In Chapter 2, we will create empathy within your classroom. In Chapter 3, we'll discuss how to teach empathy. Chapter 4 will focus on emotional intelligence and its connection to empathy. In Chapter 5, we'll develop strategies for maintaining empathy in your classroom. In Chapter 6, we'll discuss how your students can give back to society. Chapter 7 will provide you with ideas for using technology to promote empathy. Chapter 8 will provide advice for leading your school toward an empathy initiative. In the conclusion, we'll create a future vision of empathy together and discuss how to nurture empathy on a daily basis.

Each chapter concludes with discussion questions that will help you nurture empathy in your classroom, as well as questions for your students. By the end of this book, you'll guide your students into a caring world.

Timeline

It's best to develop initiatives at the beginning of the school year. But even if you have just a few weeks of school left, plan ahead for September. Everything you do matters. Even the smallest steps can make a huge impact on students' lives.

Personal and Professional Development

At the end of each chapter, you'll find writing prompts measuring your progress toward becoming a caring educator. I encourage you to get a journal and write about your experiences—from the first steps to the final results. These writing exercises will help you build a permanent record of your progress. By creating a journal, you'll create a record of empathy in your classroom.

How Will This Book Benefit Your Students?

In each chapter, you'll find writing exercises and discussion questions for your class. Students will learn to how to turn their school into a caring and compassionate place through discussions and journal activities. Empathy is both an individual adventure and a communal journey.

This book also includes journal prompts, activities, and examples of students embracing and demonstrating empathy both in school and at home. As you read this book, imagine the possibilities within your classroom and feel the spark of your creativity.

A Note About Student Quotes

Throughout this book, you'll read excerpts from reflections and essays by students. These students responded to writing prompts about empathy while taking my Composition I class at Florida Gulf Coast University during the spring of 2018. In response to writing prompts, students wrote about the influence of empathy in their lives, including moments when they witnessed empathy or acted with empathy toward another person. These reflections helped students create a more empathetic classroom and university. When appropriate, they can be shared with your students to help them reflect on their own experiences.

Chapter 1

What Is Empathy?

> Do not believe that he who seeks to comfort you
> lives untroubled among the simple and quiet words
> that sometimes do you good. His life has much dif-
> ficulty and sadness. . . . Were it otherwise, he would
> never have been able to find those words.
>
> —Rainer Maria Rilke

Where were you on September 11, 2001? This date brings back visions of horror and chaos, trauma and triumph, courage and despair that echoed across the nation. It's impossible to forget the falling buildings, fleeing people, and relatives searching endlessly for loved ones. These images are seared into our collective memories. Nearly 20 years later, I am still haunted by the fear, destruction, and memories of loved ones who died in this tragedy. Even though I did not lose a friend or relative in 9/11, my heart goes out to those who did. Why do I feel sorrow when I did not suffer immeasurable loss?

By the time we reach adulthood, we have experienced pain, suffering, and loss. We have been rejected, lost a loved one, or suffered a failure we will never forget. These experiences help us feel empathy for other people and what they are experiencing. Because I am part of the stream of humanity, I have experienced despair and pain. So I feel empathy for people impacted by 9/11.

Why is empathy important? Empathy helps us see the world from multiple viewpoints. Empathy helps us imagine the pain, joy, suffering, exhilaration, and love that other people feel, informing our choices and leading us to make connections. Empathy allows us to experience the world at a deeper level.

HISTORY AND DEFINITIONS OF EMPATHY

What is the history of empathy? When did people first look beyond their own perspectives and embrace the viewpoints of their neighbors? Although we cannot pinpoint an exact date, we can look at how the word *empathy* has evolved over the years. The term dates back to Ancient Greece, where *empatheia* was defined as "physical affection or passion." *Empatheia* derived from *pathos*, which meant "suffering or passion."

During the past 100 years, this term has evolved several times. According to Lanzoni (2015),

> The English word "empathy" came into being only about a century ago as a translation for the German psychological term *Einfühlung*, literally meaning "feeling-in." English-speaking psychologists suggested a handful of other translations for the word, including "animation," "play," "aesthetic sympathy," and "semblance." But in 1908, two psychologists from Cornell and University of Cambridge

> suggested "empathy" for *Einfühlung,* drawing on
> the Greek "em" for "in" and "pathos" for "feeling,"
> and it stuck. (para. 4)

Lanzoni (2015) further stated that empathy changed meaning again within the 20th century:

> In 1948, the experimental psychologist Rosalind
> Dymond Cartwright, in collaboration with her
> sociologist mentor, Leonard Cottrell, conducted
> some of the first tests measuring interpersonal
> empathy. In the process, she deliberately rejected
> empathy's early meaning of imaginative projection,
> and instead emphasized interpersonal connection
> as the core of the concept. (para. 6)

By the mid-20th century, empathy had evolved into its modern definition: the ability to understand another person's perspective and feelings.

There are several types of empathy: cognitive, emotional, and compassionate empathy:

- *Cognitive empathy* means understanding another person's perspective or mental state.
- *Emotional empathy* is the ability to feel another person's emotions.
- *Compassionate empathy* is feeling for another person and taking action on his or her behalf.

As educators, we must experience empathy at all three levels, but it's most critical that we experience *compassionate empathy* on a daily basis. We must understand what our students are going through and act on their behalf. For the purposes of this book, I will refer to *empathy* as a term that encompasses these three types of empathy.

Empathy helps us imagine the pain, joy, suffering, exhilaration, and love that other people feel, informing our choices and leading us to make connections.

How should we define *empathy* today? While reading this book, you will create your own definition of this term. Several existing definitions are particularly interesting to look at as you develop your own definition of empathy:

- Leonard (2019) defined empathy as "a feeling state that connects one human being to another through authentic emotional understanding" (para. 6). Leonard provided further elaboration: "Often, the person who receives empathy feels truly understood, and therefore connected to the person who understands. He or she feels far less alone in his or her predicament. This experience is healing and soothing" (para. 6).
- Lanzoni (2018) defined empathy as "our capacity to grasp and understand the mental and emotional lives of others. It is variably deemed a trained skill, a talent, or an inborn ability and accorded a psychological and moral nature" (p. 3).
- Pink (2006) defined empathy as "*feeling* with someone else, sensing what it would be like to be that person. Empathy is the stunning act of imaginative derring-do, the ultimate virtual reality experience—climbing into another's mind to experience the world from that person's perspective" (p. 159). This definition reflects the historical origins of empathy as well as a 21st-century perspective.

As you read this book, you'll realize that empathy is constantly evolving and changing, and that we all participate in this dynamic concept. By the time you finish reading, you will have created and revised your own definition of empathy.

THE JOURNEY TO EMPATHY

We cannot walk a literal mile in someone else's shoes, but we can take figurative steps toward understanding what other people are going through. An ancient metaphor states, "The journey of a thousand miles begins with a single step." No matter where we are going, we must take the first step to get there. As we journey toward empathy, we must connect with the people around us at a deeper level.

In *Gift From the Sea*, Lindbergh (1955) contemplated the common experiences of humanity. She wrote:

> Even those whose lives had appeared to be ticking imperturbably under their smiling clock-faces were often trying, like me, to evolve another rhythm with more creative pauses in it, more adjustments to their individual needs, and new and more alive relationships to themselves as well as others. (pp. 10–11)

This quote invites us to look beyond ourselves and to develop a closer relationship with those around us. We must let go of forced smiles and create authentic relationships with family, friends, and others.

The path toward empathy is like the heroic journey delineated by Campbell (1993) in *The Hero With a Thousand Faces*. In his classic book, Campbell described the archetypal hero who leaves his homeland to begin a significant journey. Away from home, the hero undergoes trials and tribulations in another land. The adventurer seeks worldly treasure and success, but he also brings knowledge back to his world. As educators, we have gone on a heroic journey through our own lives, and we have invaluable wisdom to share with our students. Can we guide our students toward becoming their best selves as they develop empathy? That depends upon if the effort we are willing to put into our teaching.

When students enter our classroom, they are beginning a heroic journey. It's easy to get so bogged down with planning lessons and grading papers that we forget our true responsibility as educators: to inspire students toward their own life journeys. Not only should we teach factual information, but we must also encourage students to pursue excellence. We can teach knowledge and empathy concurrently if we make a conscious effort to do so.

This conscious effort doesn't happen automatically. When I first started teaching, I watched students help each other in countless ways, ranging from group projects to peer editing. By the end of the semester, they expressed empathy, kindness, and compassion toward each other. Although I witnessed empathy, I didn't yet know how to teach it. For years I watched students develop empathy without participating in the process.

Still, not every student had a completely positive experience in my classroom. Most students became part of the community, but others lagged in the background, outliers within the academic landscape. How could I bring everyone into the fold in a positive way?

In 2008, I volunteered with Presidential Classroom, a high school program in Washington, DC, in which students experience academic and leadership opportunities. At the beginning of the week, Jessie, age 18, sat away from the group and was not engaged. While flying into Washington, DC, Jessie had sat next to a man who vomited several times. The airline dry-cleaned Jessie's suit but could not remove this unpleasant memory. Although I couldn't do anything about the miserable plane flight, I offered encouragement to Jessie. By the end of the week, Jessie felt comfortable with the other students. I'd shown this student empathy, but had I done enough?

There's no better example of a teacher connecting with a student than Annie Sullivan and Helen Keller. At 19 months, Helen Keller lost her hearing and sight; she could no longer understand the connection between objects and language. On April 5, 1887, Sullivan held Keller's hand under a water pump and spelled out "w-a-t-e-r" on her other hand. In *The Story of My Life*, Keller (1903/1996) wrote about this moment:

> I stood still, my whole attention fixed upon the motions of her fingers. Suddenly I felt a misty consciousness as of something forgotten—a thrill of returning thought, and somehow the mystery of language was revealed to me. I knew then that 'w-a-t-e-r' meant the wonderful cool something that was flowing over my hand. That living word awaked my soul, gave it light, hope, joy, set it free! There were barriers still, it is true, but barriers that could in time be swept away. (p. 15)

For the first time in 5 years, Keller understood language. Sullivan's commitment to empathy allowed her to share this transformative moment with her pupil. Like Annie Sullivan, we can sweep away barriers and build connections with children. But first we must think outside the box. We must go beyond the traditional curriculum and create innovative ways of teaching. We must develop connections with our students, even if they are decades removed from our own childhoods.

How can we do this? One way is to consider how our students best learn. In a personal e-mail to me, a woman who was blind recalled taking a science class in which the professor discussed the anatomy of the brain:

> I had a difficult time understanding the intricacies and connections, and I couldn't visualize the brain. What did it weigh, and how was it shaped? What did it feel like? As I struggled, the instructor removed the brain from the bottle and allowed me to hold it. I touched it, felt it, and savored the details of the magnificent structure. Finally I understood what a brain felt like. (personal communication, April 18, 2017)

Because this woman could not visualize the brain, her professor allowed her to experience the brain directly and to create her own pattern of understanding. She engaged with the organ, feeling the sutures and layout of the brain with her fingertips and developing her own understanding of its structure.

The most effective way to study empathy is by witnessing it. Several years ago my brother Brian met a young woman, Diane, from Ireland on the beach in Naples, FL. Brian and Diane both have Down syndrome, and they were able to connect over shared experiences. Later Brian received a letter from Ireland saying Diane's mother had died. Brian wrote back, "I'm so sorry to hear about your mother. The people we love stay with us forever. They remain in our hearts." In just a few words, Brian expressed his emotions in a way few people can. Reading his message, I realized empathy often appears organically. Perhaps it cannot be taught—or can it?

> We can sweep away barriers and build connections with children. But first we must think outside the box. We must go beyond the traditional curriculum and create innovative ways of teaching.

To answer this question, I decided to study empathy in a formal way. I reread several books, including Carnegie's (1981) classic text *How to Win Friends and Influence People.* Although Carnegie didn't discuss empathy directly, he provided advice for connecting with people. To connect with another person, we must see the world from his or her point of view. The book is intended to help people in business situations, but Carnegie's principles also work in the classroom.

Your conversation with a student could be the first and only time you speak with this child. Or it could be the beginning of a wonderful mentorship. Depending upon your attitude, you can positively or negatively impact a student forever.

THE POWER OF A SINGLE MOMENT

When I was in school, I had many positive interactions with teachers. But I had one notable negative encounter. During my first week of high school, I was getting changed in the girls' locker room for cross-country practice when a teacher looked over and said, "You need to leave. This is the girls' room."

I was mortified. I had short hair, and I was lanky and tall. Perhaps that is what led her to think that I did not belong there. But if I couldn't change in the girls' room, where could I get dressed?

I forgot this incident until 2013, when I was in training for Safe Zone. The Safe Zone Project sponsors regular trainings to help professors, staff, and students develop a better understanding of the LGBTQ community, as well as gender and sexual identities. During our training session, our guide discussed how some students might feel being kicked out of the bathroom.

Until that moment, I had just been attending a training session to help students. But as we discussed students getting kicked out of restrooms, time collapsed. They were talking about something that had happened to me! Suddenly I felt empathy for students with different gender orientations, particularly for people who had gone through the same humiliating experience that I had.

What did I learn from this experience? Every time teachers interact with students, we make an impact. Teachers make a lasting impact (either positive or negative) depending upon how they converse with students. Think back to the classic Tennyson (1842) poem "Ulysses," in which the main character comments, "I am a part of all that I have met." Every time you step into your classroom, you are part of those students' lives forever. Why not inspire your students toward excellence?

As educators, our influence extends far beyond our classrooms. As Christa McAuliffe once said, "I touch the future. I teach." McAuliffe is a wonderful example of a teacher who continues to make a positive impact on students more than 30 years after her death. Who can forget the woman who created curriculum to teach from outer space? We must become caring people. We must grow in dynamic ways as educators. We must develop psychically, intellectually, and spiritually to become the best teachers we can be. This involves change at every level.

Is it possible to continue to grow as an educator, even if you have been teaching for many years? When my brother Andrew was 10 years old, he took piano lessons with Dorothy Guion (who was in her 90s at the time) in Springfield, MA. Mrs. Guion required all of her students to study classical piano. That summer Andrew campaigned to play "The Entertainer," a song that did not fit into Mrs. Guion's "classical music" classification. But Mrs. Guion let him study this piece anyway, so that he would become more engaged with music. As my brother learned this piece, Mrs. Guion gave precise instructions about the tone and the speed of the song, including how individual notes should be played. Andrew had a difficult time living up to her standards.

One afternoon Mrs. Guion explained, "When I was a little girl, I heard Scott Joplin play this piece. I want you to play it exactly the same way." Finally Andrew understood why Mrs. Guion had been so careful with her instructions. Mrs. Guion became a better teacher when she realized the importance of letting students choose their own music, but she managed to maintain her strict standards in different ways.

> We must develop psychically, intellectually, and spiritually to become the best teachers we can be. This involves change at every level.

EMPATHY AND INTELLIGENCE

What is the connection between empathy and intelligence? When Mayer and Salovey (1993) created the term *emotional intelligence*, they believed it was a mental aptitude, "one that assists in intellectual processing" (p. 439). They believed that

> different types of people may be more or less emotionally intelligent. Emotionally intelligent people may be more aware of their own feelings and those of others. They may be more open to positive and negative aspects of internal experience, better able to label them, and when appropriate, communicate them. (p. 440)

Mayer and Salovey also believed that emotional intelligence overlaps with Gardner's (1983/2011) concept of interpersonal intelligence. (See Chapter 4 for an in-depth discussion of emotional intelligence.)

Multiple Intelligences

Although schools reward people who score highly on linguistic and logical-mathematical tests, our framework of intelligence has broadened. Gardner's (1983/2011) *Frames of Mind: The Theory of Multiple Intelligences* outlines several kinds of intelligence. When I first read this book in graduate school, I could suddenly see beyond linear intelligence to other types of intelligence; friends who excelled on the basketball court had kinesthetic intelligence, while standouts on the student council exhibited interpersonal intelligence. Gardner delineated the intelligences to include the following categories:

- linguistic,
- logical-mathematical,
- visual-spatial,
- musical,
- bodily-kinesthetic,
- interpersonal, and
- intrapersonal.

In 1995, Gardner made the case for including naturalistic intelligence. Four years later (Gardner, 1999), he suggested including existential intelligence in the multiple intelligences theory.

This year I reread *Frames of Mind* (Gardner, 1983/2011) from a different perspective: What role does empathy play in intelligence? Is it possible to teach empathy? In the book, Gardner defined different types of intelligence, including interpersonal and intrapersonal intelligence:

- *Interpersonal intelligence* is closely connected to empathy; it refers to being sensitive to other peoples' feelings and needs. Salespeople, teachers, counselors, and social workers are perfect examples of people with interpersonal intelligence.
- *Intrapersonal intelligence* refers to understanding our own emotions. When we understand ourselves, we relate to other people better, so intra- and interpersonal intelligence naturally completement each other.

Although Gardner (1983/2011) included existential and moral intelligence in his list of possible intelligences, he did not have a separate category for empathy intelligence. However, Gardner recognized people who ask big questions (existential intelligence) and those who act morally in difficult situations (moral intelligence). These kinds of intelligence are directly connected to empathy.

People of all intelligence levels can express empathy toward others. Other intelligences (as outlined by Gardner, 1983/2011) require finesse (bodily-kinesthetic), a certain level of IQ (logical-mathematical), the skill to decipher codes (linguistic), and the ability to see relationships (visual-spatial). Empathy cuts across economic and intelligence levels. If you are willing to put the effort in, you can develop a high level of empathy.

IQ and Empathy

The relationship between empathy and intelligence is complicated. Those who score well on IQ tests would fail an empathy test if they were unable to relate to people who have different life experiences. Most intelligence tests measure how well a person analyzes patterns and codes. A person who scores highly on an IQ test can answer questions quickly but can't necessarily understand another person's perspective. Many gifted people demonstrate empathy toward others, but there's no clear correlation between IQ and empathy.

In essence, intelligent people are capable of developing high levels of empathy, but it doesn't happen automatically. Empathy takes effort, training, and work just like any other talent. With an understanding of the self (intrapersonal intelligence), a child can develop understanding of other people (interpersonal intelligence) as well. When a child connects with other people, he becomes a caring person. A child with both a high IQ and emotional intelligence has the potential to develop into a world-class leader.

Here's the good news: You don't need an IQ of 180 to experience empathy. You don't have to be Einstein to help a neighbor shovel her driveway or to volunteer for a Special Olympics track team. You don't need to be rich to demonstrate concern toward other people. You can give time, energy, and internal resources. Empathy simply requires being open-minded and understanding other people. Samantha, a student in my composition class, reflected on the power of demonstrating empathy:

> When my best friend found out her uncle had cancer, she needed a shoulder to cry on. I was there for her. I told her everything would be all right.

Samantha not only demonstrated empathy at a crucial moment, but she also reflected about it in the essay she wrote. Empathy is being there for someone going through a difficult experience. Even if you haven't experienced what that person is going through, you are able to imagine what she feels.

TAKING THE TIME

Empathy takes time to develop and to discover within oneself. In *An American Childhood*, Dillard (2009) described her growing consciousness and how it took her many years to become fully awake within the world: "I woke in bits, like all children, piecemeal over the years. I discovered myself and the world, and forgot them, and discovered them again" (p. 11). We enter a world that is constantly in motion, and it takes time to negotiate the language and cultural barriers. A growing consciousness does not happen all at once but takes place over the course of several years. In the classic book *How the Grinch Stole Christmas!* (Seuss, 1957), the Grinch's heart grows several sizes in just a few moments. In real life it takes years to develop a sense of empathy and express it toward another person.

What could be more meaningful than expressing empathy? In *Social Intelligence*, Goleman (2006) wrote, "Every interaction has an emotional subtext. Along with whatever else we are doing, we can make each other feel a little better, or even a lot better, or a little worse—or a lot worse" (p. 14). Social intelligence impacts social interactions and determines how well people connect with each other. Examples of empathetic interactions include the following:

- Missy Franklin's neighbors decorated her lawn with words of encouragement and love after the 2016 Olympics.
- Harriet Beecher Stowe wrote a novel, *Uncle Tom's Cabin*, highlighting the evils of slavery.
- Harriet Tubman led thousands of slaves to freedom along the Underground Railroad.

- Wendy Kopp (2003) founded Teach for America to bring the best college graduates into inner city and rural schools around America.

Empathy is a skill that can be developed, not a fixed ability. Sometimes surviving a difficult experience can promote empathy. On October 12, 2018, Princess Eugenie of Great Britain wore an open-backed wedding gown to highlight the scars from her scoliosis surgery in early adolescence. She stated, "I think you can change the way beauty is, and you can show people your scars and I think it's really special to stand up for that" (ITV Report, 2018). With this act, Eugenie demonstrated empathy toward people around the world who are dealing with this health issue.

We all have the potential to discover how to relate to the people who cross our paths. As educators, we nurture students with knowledge and understanding. We can help children develop an emotional connection with each other so that they can later connect with people from all walks of life. All children have the capacity to learn empathy in our classrooms.

MEASURING EMPATHY

How do you measure kindness and sensitivity? How can you document a child's empathy in comparison to that of other students across the country? Empathy is difficult to measure with certainty.

Educators are good at measuring objectives and assessing performances across a wide panorama of human activity. If we want to test a student's mathematical ability, we give questions with specific answers. If a student runs competitively, we compare her times to other high school students across the country. If we want to see whether a child's vocabulary is improving, we give her a test.

Similarly, one of the best ways to measure empathy is in a situational context. In 2012, Arden McGrath collapsed 20 m away from the finish line of the Ohio Division III girls' track championship. Instead of running past her, Meghan Vogel carried her opponent to the finish line. Although neither girl won the race, they won the hearts of the people watching. Some moments can't be measured by time, and some races are won by connecting with others, not by crossing the finish line.

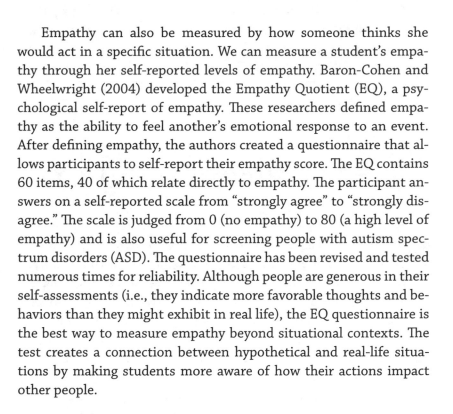

All children have the capacity to learn empathy in our classrooms.

Empathy can also be measured by how someone thinks she would act in a specific situation. We can measure a student's empathy through her self-reported levels of empathy. Baron-Cohen and Wheelwright (2004) developed the Empathy Quotient (EQ), a psychological self-report of empathy. These researchers defined empathy as the ability to feel another's emotional response to an event. After defining empathy, the authors created a questionnaire that allows participants to self-report their empathy score. The EQ contains 60 items, 40 of which relate directly to empathy. The participant answers on a self-reported scale from "strongly agree" to "strongly disagree." The scale is judged from 0 (no empathy) to 80 (a high level of empathy) and is also useful for screening people with autism spectrum disorders (ASD). The questionnaire has been revised and tested numerous times for reliability. Although people are generous in their self-assessments (i.e., they indicate more favorable thoughts and behaviors than they might exhibit in real life), the EQ questionnaire is the best way to measure empathy beyond situational contexts. The test creates a connection between hypothetical and real-life situations by making students more aware of how their actions impact other people.

TESTING AND REWARDS

By the time students enter the third grade, they have taken standardized tests that determine their reading levels, math prowess, and how they compare academically to other children across the country. But it's impossible to measure other important qualities that people need in life—empathy, kindness, or creativity—through a multiple-choice test.

As teachers, we are trained in classroom management, crafting lesson plans, and developing syllabi. We're evaluated based on how well our students take standardized tests. We don't give students extra credit for providing words of comfort to a friend, helping a student with a disability prepare for a sports event, or assisting a classmate with a worksheet. Nor can these acts be quantified on a resume or college application. Although many high schools require community service for graduation, it's difficult to evaluate what students learn through these experiences. One child can have a life-changing experience, while another student may just fulfill a graduation requirement.

It is difficult to measure what students learn from life experiences and how these insights impact their lives. In *A Sense of Where You Are*, McPhee (1978) wrote about Bill Bradley: "Bradley says that when he was seventeen he came to realize that life was much longer than a few winters of basketball. He is quite serious in his application of the game, but he has wider interests and, particularly, bigger ambitions" (p. 13). After graduating from Princeton, Bradley played for the Nets and eventually became a U.S. senator. In this capacity, he served the needs of the greater public. Bradley created experiences that impacted his life beyond what he or his teachers originally had measured.

In *Drive: The Surprising Truth About What Motivates Us*, Pink (2009) delineated the drawbacks to giving students external rewards, which:

- limit intrinsic motivation,
- hamper good conduct,

- squash creativity, and
- encourage a short-term thinking pattern.

People get internal satisfaction from helping others, and this intrinsic award is far more valuable than receiving a plaque at a ceremony. Although school administrators don't often reward empathy with certificates or awards, it may be the most important thing a child learns in school.

We continue to reward students based upon self-achievement. On tests, we award students according to a zero-sum game and penalize children who study with others indirectly (i.e., if your friends score as well as you did on the final, your A is no longer as valuable as it would be if you achieved it alone). Why do we grade achievement based on a zero-sum game? In real-life situations, scientists and researchers work in teams. Many famous scientists, including Thomas Edison, had a team of researchers working with them.

So, how can we reward empathy? Teaching a child to care about other people can be difficult. It's challenging to assess or grade empathy within a traditional rubric. When students engage in caring acts, they rarely receive credit. Empathy is an elusive quality to judge, grade, or assess with a rubric.

However, students can learn content knowledge and empathy at the same time. I remember the teachers who covered important content in a way that allowed me to become emotionally involved. I cannot recall the facts and figures I studied in an astronomy class in college, but I'll never forget how our professor took us on a tour of the skyline. He brought the wonders of the universe into his lectures. The "reward" for students who reach higher levels of empathy may be the experience itself, which they can draw from and build upon in the future.

CONNECTING WITH YOUR STUDENTS

As classrooms grow more diverse, teachers may not know the best ways to connect with students' backgrounds. According to the Association of American Colleges and Universities (2019), in 2017 the United States population was 18% Hispanic, 12.3% African American, 1.9% people with more than one racial background, .7% American Indian or Alaska Native, and .3% Native Hawaiian. Among the youngest generations, this diversity is even more apparent. You may work with students who live on reservations, whose parents immigrated to the United States, or who identify with more than one race. That can be exciting, but it comes with the responsibility of learning how to teach these diverse populations.

Students may come from different backgrounds than you, but, above all, they want to be appreciated and respected in your classroom. You can be the teacher who guides students to a deeper understanding of human nature. You *can* relate to every student. Students will appreciate even the smallest efforts you make to connect with them. Sometimes educators focus on discipline rather than on finding out why students are misbehaving in the first place. If students feel respected, they are less likely to misbehave (see the example dialogues in Chapter 2). You'll teach to a community of learners, not to an adversarial audience.

Bringing empathy into your classroom isn't easy. No matter how much effort you make, you can't guarantee success. You cannot control someone else's behavior, nor can you legislate the way children behave outside your classroom. But you can always treat your students with respect and encourage your students to treat each other with respect. Many students are isolated from their peer group and become the butt of jokes. Although educators have worked hard to eradicate bullying, more work needs to be done. In *Anne of Green Gables*, Montgomery (1908/2014) wrote, "There's a world of difference between being on the inside looking out and being on the outside looking in." All students must feel like they are part of the class, and that they aren't on the outside looking in.

Let's travel back in time. Do you remember your school experiences? Maybe you ate lunch with friends every day. You were invited to birthday parties during the year and pool parties during the summer. But you were also left out a few times, and it hurt your feelings. Now think about the students in your class who didn't receive invites to any events. What happened to these children? Because of Facebook and other social media platforms, we can see how loners turned out. Some former loners lead healthy, successful lives today, but we never hear from others. Where are these people today?

Now, look around your classroom. There are kids who don't have a table to sit at during lunch or friends to play with during recess. There are students who don't receive invites to a party all year long. There are children who would love to join in a kickball game at recess but are too shy to ask. How can you bring these outliers into the group? Children know it's important to reach out to kids outside the main group. When you make an effort to bring all of your students into your class, kids will follow your example. When you act with empathy, your students will, too.

> **Students may come from different backgrounds than you, but, above all, they want to be appreciated and respected in your classroom.**

PURSUING EXCELLENCE IN EMPATHY

Educators assess excellence within a language arts or mathematics classroom based upon skills that can easily be measured, but it's far more difficult translating a student's empathetic qualities into a skill. Is there a systematic way to transform a talent like empathy into a world-class ability?

Duckworth and Gross (2014) provided an equation for how talent can be translated into achievement: "Talent x Effort = Skill" (p. 44). When you put effort into a field that you are talented in, you will achieve something with your newly developed skills. Duckworth and Gross's equation translates well across many areas, including empathy. Although empathy is not typically quantified, there are ways to develop this ability. Many talents require specific skills, but empathy only requires learning to consider others' feelings and perspectives. You don't have to throw a baseball at 92 mph or run a mile in under 6 minutes to excel.

In *Final Exam: A Surgeon's Reflections on Mortality*, Chen (2007) wrote about empathy from a surgeon's perspective. Chen felt that she was trained to save lives and to view death as the ultimate enemy. In reality, death is an integral part of every doctor's practice, but very few doctors receive training in empathy or assisting their patients through difficult times. When a terminally ill patient is dying, doctors usually leave the scene, sometimes feeling a sense of failure. One day Chen experienced an epiphany when she witnessed a doctor approach an elderly woman whose husband was dying. Rather than avoiding the situation, this doctor sat beside the woman and explained what was happening. This doctor developed empathy to the highest level, and was able to offer words of support at a critical time.

Teachers may never have the opportunity to make a life-or-death impact, but we can still develop empathy to a high level. Although empathy may not require specific cognitive or physical skills, you have to understand other people's feelings, which is far more challenging. You have to apply a concentrated effort over an extended period of time. But all of this effort will be worth it in the end. You could be the person who makes a huge impact on another person's life, just like the doctor in Chen's (2007) example did. You may be the only person who can help someone through a difficult situation.

Students appreciate the difficulty of developing empathy. Many students admit that it is difficult to step into another person's experience and to truly understand his perspective. How do you see outside your own perspective? It might be helpful to use Duckworth and Gross's (2014) definition as a starting point: "Talent x Effort = Skill" (p. 44). However, for our purposes, let's replace "talent" with "sensitivity":

$$\text{Sensitivity x Effort} = \text{Empathy}$$

Sensitivity (the awareness of the emotions and needs of others) and effort culminate in higher levels of empathy. Sensitivity is required to develop empathy in the first place. Without effort and discipline, empathy remains a tendency, not a well-developed skill. When people fine-tune this ability, it emerges as a talent.

The Power of Practice

In *Outliers: The Story of Success*, Gladwell (2008) discussed the concept of 10,000 hours of practice to reach world-class expertise. People who put the time in are more likely to achieve excellence, and luck plays a critical part in the outcome. The difference between someone who attains superb talent and someone who becomes proficient is the hours of practice. Talent may be overrated, so it's best to look at life circumstances and opportunities when studying success.

James Henshon (2019), a student at Roxbury Latin School, recently gave a speech about practicing free throws:

> When I watch basketball on TV, I'm always surprised when a player misses a free throw. They are supposed to be "free" right? But, when I am the one in a clutch situation, too often I miss. Though shooting 100% on free throws might not be possible, the only way to improve your percentage is to

> practice a lot. You have to practice until the proper
> motion is completely muscle memory. This means
> repetition and more repetition. Dribble, dribble,
> spin, focus on where the rim meets the blackboard,
> dribble once more, shoot. Doing this thousands
> and thousands of times is the only way to improve
> my chances in those clutch moments. (p. 9)

When we practice a motion or an emotional connection thousands of times, we are able to perform when our skill is needed. Whether this means being there for a friend whose father is diagnosed with cancer or helping a stranger find her wallet, we know what to do in the moment. We are prepared for those "clutch" moments in life.

Abraham Lincoln is a perfect example of an empathetic life developed through practice. At the age of 7, Lincoln lost his mother. Later he lost his beloved stepmother and younger brother. But Lincoln was deeply passionate about education and studied to be a lawyer. Eventually he married Marry Todd Lincoln and they settled in Springfield, IL. The Lincolns had four sons, and lost one of their boys to tuberculosis. As president, Lincoln watched over a nation immersed in the Civil War. In November 1864, Lincoln wrote a very moving letter to Mrs. Bixby, who had lost five sons on the battlefield. In order to write this letter, Lincoln needed writing skills and life experience. More importantly, he needed empathy, which he had developed at a high level during the course of his life through sensitivity and effort. Empathy requires dedication and practice, just like any other ability. Students can study the development of empathy across the life span in luminaries like Princess Diana and Mother Theresa.

Several years ago, I visited the John F. Kennedy Presidential Library and Museum in Boston, MA. Walking through the library, I realized that Kennedy's life is a study of empathy. As a child, he was sensitive and compassionate. As a congressman, Kennedy wrote a Pulitzer prize-winning book, *Profiles in Courage*, about political leaders who had sacrificed personal benefits for the good of the country. Later Kennedy emerged as an international leader. On the surface, he led a very privileged life. He attended Choate Rosemary Hall and Harvard University before serving in the Congress and Senate. But he never forgot his Irish Catholic roots or the people he grew up with.

President Kennedy's concern for others did not develop on a linear plane. Like many elusive qualities, empathy is a skill that can be fine-tuned over a lifetime. When students come to our classrooms, they have different levels of empathy. They bring unique personalities and qualities. That's why we must encourage every student we work with—developing empathy can take a lifetime.

FINAL THOUGHTS

Empathy is the most meaningful and challenging concept you can teach your students. Even if you don't see immediate results, keep trying. Empathy can be the difference between a rewarding or floundering career, or between a meaningful life and simply going through the motions. In building empathy, you're creating something that will extend years into the future.

When students enter your classroom, they bring a variety of experiences with them. The common thread in their lives is you. You have something invaluable and precious to offer your students. What they learn about empathy may be far more valuable than anything else they study in your classroom.

DISCUSSION QUESTIONS

For Teachers

1. Describe a moment when you showed concern for another person. What were the circumstances, and how did you act? What did you learn from showing empathy?
2. How can you develop concern for your students at a higher level? What can you do to become a better teacher today?
3. How would you expand or revise the definitions of empathy shared in this chapter? Create a new definition based on your knowledge and experience.

For Students

1. How has empathy impacted your life experiences?
2. Can empathy be developed with practice? How could you practice empathy this week?
3. Does someone have to be smart to be empathetic? Explain your answer.

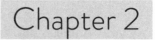

Chapter 2

How Can You Create an Empathetic Classroom?

Leadership is about empathy.

—Oprah Winfrey

What can you do to build a classroom in which people feel genuine concern for each other? Here's the good news. Every day, millions of people express empathy toward each other. Since the beginning of time, people have demonstrated kindness toward each other in myriad ways. As an educator, you can promote this tendency toward empathy in a natural and holistic way. After all, the world is filled with empathy. Why shouldn't empathy flow into your classroom if it exists everywhere else?

Empathy happens in a variety of contexts. For example, during her tenure as First Lady, Michelle Obama planted a vegetable garden to promote healthy eating. Mrs. Obama invited children from the local community to participate, and the garden became an outreach project. By showing empathy, the First Lady made a huge impact on the lives of people around the country.

You can plant empathy, too. Every time you step into your classroom, you can bring empathy to your students. You can transform children's lives with kind words and actions. Your students will carry your kindness into the cafeteria, other classrooms, and their own homes. Everything you do matters, and your influence extends into the future.

Wait a second, you might be thinking. You've always made an effort to treat students kindly and to make sure that they treat each other with respect. Why do you need to implement empathy? Why turn a natural concept into a formal initiative?

Building empathy is an ongoing process, and it begins with small steps. You can achieve success if you work on empathy every day, rather than waiting for it to happen naturally. With small acts of empathy, you can plant kindness in your school. Students will act with concern toward each other when they realize how important it is to you.

CREATING A CARING CLASSROOM

As you build empathy into your lesson plans, you lay the foundation for a caring world. Empathy isn't an abstract concept; it's a living entity. Empathy must happen *every day* in your classroom, not just at the beginning of the year.

Won't this take a lot of time? Running a classroom is one of the most complicated responsibilities you have. You teach, counsel, and comfort dozens of students during the course of a single day. Can you build a caring classroom along with all of the other duties you must perform? Perhaps the better question is: Can you afford *not* to build a caring classroom? As Eldridge Cleaver once said, "There is no more neutrality in the world. You either have to be part of the solution, or you're going to be part of the problem." If we teach without empathy, we will have a devastating impact on society.

Imagine a world without empathy. It's a place where people spend all of their discretionary income on themselves and never help a person in need. It's a land where people fail to understand other people's viewpoints or help strangers in distress. Would you want to live in such a place?

With small acts of empathy, you can plant kindness in your school.

Let's consider what happens when people don't care at all. In Lowry's (1993) *The Giver*, Jonas comes of age in a place where people are numb to emotions and unable to feel pain. The boy receives memories as part of his training to be a giver. Eventually Jonas moves to a land where people experience emotions instead of remaining in a world devoid of feelings. How can we stop *The Giver* from becoming our future? Empathy doesn't happen overnight. Creating a caring classroom is the first step toward making a difference in the world. By taking small steps every day, your influence will extend to your entire school.

STEPS FOR BUILDING EMPATHY

There are several steps involved in building empathy (see Figure 1). The following sections provide guidance and examples for conducting each step.

1. Introduce the word *empathy* to your class and have students brainstorm what it might mean.
2. Have each student create a personal definition of empathy.
3. Have students write about a moment when they experienced empathy—either as a beneficiary or a giver of empathy to another person.
4. Model empathy through your actions and words.
5. Discuss empathy with your students in the context of everyday lessons.
6. Keep an open line of communication going in your classroom.
7. Encourage students to write about and discuss their struggles with empathy.
8. Ask students to apply empathy in their volunteer or leadership experiences outside of the classroom.

Figure 1. Eight steps for developing empathy in the classroom.

Step 1: Introduce Empathy

Discuss the word *empathy* with your class and have students brainstorm definitions of this term. Tell students,

> Today we're going to talk about empathy. Using your class dictionaries, look up *empathy* and write down how this term is defined.

Minutes later, you can lead a discussion with the following prompt:

> Now that you've looked up empathy in the dictionary, let's talk about how we use empathy in our lives. Who would like to share?

Step 2: Have Students Create a Personal Definition

When students describe empathy in their own words, they'll see its impact on their daily lives. You can start with a simple statement:

> Create your own personal definition of *empathy* that reflects the historical origins of the word. Write a definition and explanation of this term in your journal.

The kinds of definitions students conceptualize will depend upon their experiences with other people. See the example definitions created by students in Figure 2. When asked to define *empathy* in his own words in a class discussion, a student in my class stated, "Empathy is stepping into another person's shoes and trying to see the world from his point of view." Later in this same discussion, another student stated, "Empathy is relating to someone's emotions, whether or not you've experienced their specific situation." These definitions demonstrate students connecting to the concept through their own experiences.

In response to this assignment, Jamie wrote a longer response:

> Empathy comes from the Greek word *empatheia*, which means affection, and the root word *path* means to suffer. Today empathy means perceiving other peoples' emotions and imagining what someone else is feeling. Empathy means placing yourself in a situation and thinking about how you would react. Empathy has always been important to our evolutionary history as a species. We must be sensitive to the needs of those around us. Our species depends on collaboration. It is beneficial if we help others, and empathy is the first step in taking action. Humans are not the only species to show em-

---

WHAT IS EMPATHY?

Caring for other people.

Standing in someone else's shoes.

Trying to see where another
person is coming from.

Thinking about other people and
how they see the world.

Doing my best to be a caring
classmate and friend.

Figure 2. Student definitions of empathy.

---

pathy; this ability is seen in many mammals and can
be attributed to the rise in number of registered
emotional support animals.

As students delineate empathy in their own words, the concept
will come alive in your classroom.

Step 3: Have Students Write About an Empathy Moment

Have students write about a moment when they experience empathy—either as a beneficiary or a giver of empathy to another person. The following is a writing prompt you can use with your class:

Describe a time when you experienced empathy
because of someone's kind act, or a moment when

you demonstrated concern toward another person. What did this moment mean to you?

Students find this exercise empowering, because they can share their thoughts and feelings on the page. Jamie wrote:

> I am an empathetic person. I analyze situations and think about how others feel and how I would feel if I were in their place. From a young age, my parents taught me to help someone in need in any way that I can, even with something as simple as sharing a snack with a classmate.

Step 4: Model Empathy Through Your Actions and Words

Treat every student with respect. For example, you don't have to give full credit for a late assignment, but at least give the student some credit for finishing his work. Make a point of including all of your students in the group, not just those who speak up and take charge. When you assign group projects, make sure all students are included in groups and working productively. Little steps can go a long way toward showing students the importance of empathy. When you model empathy, your students will demonstrate concern toward each other.

This step is more like an ongoing series of actions that show students how they might also become stakeholders in creating a caring classroom. Students must believe empathy is important and must show concern for each other. In *The Structure of Scientific Revolutions*, Kuhn (1962/2012) stated that revolutions occur when a critical mass of people adhere to a particular theory. Without the support of people, this theory will not become the "truth." In a comparable way, an educational initiative has little influence without the support of the entire class.

Step 5: Discuss Empathy in the Context of Everyday Lessons

Sharing a book with your students is a great way to launch a discussion. Small children enjoy reading *Leo the Late Bloomer*, which features a little tiger who can't read, write, or keep pace with other little tigers. Leo's parents are patient, however, and eventually Leo blossoms. For elementary school students, reading *The One and Only Ivan* together is a wonderful way to discuss empathy in a real-life situation. This book teaches the importance of developing a community. *Where the Red Fern Grows*, the story about two dogs that save a boy's life, is a great model of empathy for junior high school students. Reading a book together can be meaningful because it creates a shared intellectual and emotional experience.

In addition to book studies, you can consider empathy while learning about historical figures and events related to any subject you teach. No matter what subject areas you teach, continue to discuss empathy with your students so that the concept remains fresh in their memory. More ideas for infusing empathy in your lessons can be found in Chapter 3.

Step 6: Keep an Open Line of Communication

Bring students together as a larger group for activities, discussions, and other activities, rather than having students sort into self-selected groups. You may want to do "empathy checks" to see how students are progressing with this concept, particularly after the first weeks of the year. To conduct an empathy check, have students work on the following writing prompt individually:

> This year we've developed an empathy initiative in our class. What have you learned about empathy so far? Have we developed into an empathetic class? How can we show more concern for each other? Please write 1–2 paragraphs about this issue.

Students must continue to write and reflect on empathy. Not only must they have experiences with empathy, but they must also reflect about it through written exercises on a regular basis.

Step 7: Encourage Students to Write About and Discuss Their Struggles

Here is a prompt for a classroom discussion or journal response about struggling with empathy:

> Sometimes it's difficult to show empathy toward people we don't know. How can we feel empathy for people who have different life experiences and backgrounds than ourselves? Write one paragraph in response to this question.

In response, Erin wrote,

> It is hard to act with empathy toward others, mostly to people I don't know. I feel empathy toward my friends, but showing empathy sometimes makes me uncomfortable. It's difficult relating to a person if you have not had the same life experiences.

When Erin wrote this statement in response to a writing prompt about demonstrating empathy to people who are different than we are, I decided the best response was to have a class discussion about this topic.

We used this question as a launching pad for a class discussion about empathy. Students discussed how to express empathy toward people they did not connect with. Erin added to the conversation by stating that it takes more effort, but it is worth taking the extra step to relate to people. This discussion was helpful for Erin because she realized that other students felt the same way that she did.

Step 8: Apply Empathy in Volunteer or Leadership Experiences

Your students must take the caring attitude developed in the classroom into the landscape of their lives. They must demonstrate concern toward people in the outside world. When children become engaged in activity, they redefine empathy in a 21st-century world. Students will then bring their unique ideas back into your classroom.

Have students write about these volunteer experiences. Whether they have volunteered in a soup kitchen, tutored a friend, babysat a younger sibling, or helped out at a pet shelter, students accumulate many impactful experiences. For example, Molly, age 18, volunteered to work at a Planned Parenthood facility where she helped to escort young women inside:

> I have a distinct memory of escorting a young woman into the building on her procedure day with close to 30 protesters lining the street the clinic is located on. She was a scared, young woman going in on her own while strangers antagonized her from a few feet away. For me, it was a moment of sheer amazement not only that these people had the audacity to say these harsh critiques, but also her mental strength. She never looked at them or let them know how scared she was, even though I could sense it in her eyes and body language. I felt so badly for her as she was already doing something life changing, but also had to feel the wrath of these God-fearing people. What could be more difficult than what she was going through?

Molly developed and demonstrated empathy in this situation. By the end of this experience, Molly had a greater appreciation for the bravery of the young woman who was suffering humiliation and adversity walking into the clinic.

Another student, Luke, developed an appreciation for empathy while leading his band in high school. He wrote:

> When I was captain of the drumline in my high school, one of the drummers broke three of his toes and was wearing a boot. Carrying his drum and marching caused him pain. Empathizing with his difficulty and knowing that he had no control over the broken toes, I had the line come inside and play in place with the drums on stands so that we were still practicing music, but the drummer with the broken toes would not be uncomfortable, and his healing would not be compromised.

Not only did Luke understand empathy, but he also thought through a difficult situation and acted in the best interest of the entire band.

You can be a force of empathy inside and outside your classroom. You can read a book with your class, volunteer for a food drive, or help your students understand this concept through class discussions. Show concern for others rather than simply talking about it. Students must think beyond their own needs and care about other people. When you create a caring community, you'll see students expressing empathy when you least expect it.

HELPING STUDENTS DEVELOP A VISION OF THEIR FUTURE

When children step into your classroom, they are budding scholars, writers, actors, artists, athletes, and magicians. Outside school, your students are brothers, sisters, nieces, nephews, children, cousins, and grandchildren. Your students may not have life plans yet, but they have great potential.

Although it may not be wise to direct a child toward a specific career plan, it's never too early to ask someone what kind of person she wants to be. When asked their career plans, young children often mention becoming a teacher, policeman, or firefighter. Wouldn't it be useful to ask students to develop a vision of what kind of person they want to be and what steps they must take to get there?

By the time they reach high school, students are considering college and career plans, but what kind of people will they become? Ask your students to develop a vision of their future. Help your students think about their character growth and what they hope to accomplish beyond career plans. To construct this activity, begin with the following assignment:

> Draw a picture of your future self. Think beyond a physical description. How might you show yourself being a kind and sharing person who makes the world a better place? What can you do today to become that person?

As students complete this activity, they will consider not just what they want to study or pursue as a career, but also what kind of people they want to become. This self-portrait will become a vision of their future.

What visions will your students develop? When asked to write about the importance of empathy and how it really matters in our lives, a student, Christopher, wrote:

> Being able to empathize is very important for human interaction and social skills. If you go to your friend's father's funeral and cannot empathize, you will feel very out of place not being sad with everyone around you. The reason people cry for the loss

of a friend's family member is they empathize. In the future, I will develop higher levels of empathy and stronger connections with other people.

Through working on this exercise, Chris contemplated his own level of empathy. Instead of just writing about a moment in time, he embraced his future empathetic self.

PROMOTING GENEROSITY

What does it mean to be generous? Does it mean giving your time, money, and resources? Many children receive generosity in the form of love and attention from their parents and relatives. As children grow up, they must learn how to give back to society.

> Years from now, students won't remember which books were on your shelves or how your room was decorated. But they'll never forget how they felt in your presence.

We must teach children generosity. Feeling empathy is the first step, but generosity requires giving and caring in a meaningful way. When students think about other people, they become more thoughtful. The steps mentioned earlier in this section can lead to friendships and greater connections between classmates. When students realize the impact of empathy, they are more likely to be generous.

Expressing generosity can be difficult in social situations. Students may not want to hand out valentines to everyone in their class. Children may wish to invite only their closest friends to a birthday party. In many situations, kids gravitate toward people they feel most comfortable with. This leaves some students left out of the mix, on the outskirts of the circle. We must help students widen their circle of friends.

It's difficult when we learn about some children never receiving invites to parties or events. What should we do? We can't force students to be inclusive, even though a single action could make a huge difference in another student's life. But we *can* encourage kids to reach out with generosity to each other and take the first steps toward creating a caring environment.

CREATING EMPATHETIC MOMENTS

Teachers fill their classrooms with supplies at the beginning of each year. They want their classrooms to be optimal learning places, filled with technological resources. It's wonderful to have a high-tech classroom, but the interactions between people are far more important. Years from now, students won't remember which books were on your shelves or how your room was decorated. But they'll never forget how they felt in your presence.

Think back to your own school years. Close your eyes and remember the teachers who had the most impact on you. Maybe they were excited about the content they were teaching, or they brought every student into a discussion. Can you replicate these qualities in your own classroom? Can you be the teacher whom students remember decades later?

To create a positive impact, you need a game plan.

Reaching Individual Students

Let's take a look at a sample dialogue in which a teacher promotes empathy in her classroom.

Mrs. Watson:	Where is your homework, Andy?
Andy:	I didn't finish it.
Mrs. Watson:	What happened?
Andy:	My father went to the emergency room last night.
Mrs. Watson:	Oh, no. I hope he's okay.
Andy:	It was stomach digestion issues. But we thought he was having a heart attack.
Mrs. Watson:	Well, I hope he's doing better. I can see why you forgot your homework.
Andy:	Thanks for being so understanding, Mrs. Watson.

Take a look at the dialogue, and you'll see that Mrs. Watson begins by asking for Andy's homework; however, rather than chastising him, she wants to find out *why* he hasn't completed the work. Her intent is to find out what happened, and she listens to Andy. In this moment, Andy needs support far more than a detention for not completing his homework.

Group Work

Now, let's look at an empathy dialogue between three students working on a group project:

John:	What's wrong with you, Debbie? Why can't you get the right answer?

Debbie:	I typed the wrong numbers into my calculator.
John:	Can't you see that 20 + 25 doesn't equal 65?
Debbie:	Well, at least you found the mistake.
Jeff:	What matters is that we found the mistake before we turned our project in. We're working together on this, and it's important that we double-check our answers. That's why we work as a team.
John:	Okay, I guess that makes sense. Let's solve these problems together.

At the beginning of this dialogue, John chastises Debbie because she added two numbers together incorrectly. She's already embarrassed when Jeff steps in. He emphasizes the importance of working as a group, not as individuals in this project. By standing up for Debbie in a nonconfrontational matter, Jeff creates an empathetic group project scenario. Eventually John realizes it's okay to make mistakes, and that the group can solve problems together.

You are responsible for your classroom—the good and the bad. Let's make this year the best academic experience your students will ever have. It doesn't matter what grade you teach or what subject matter. As you create a caring environment, think of this a holistic process. It may take an entire year to get there. But if you work every day, you'll watch empathy emerge naturally.

Bullying

Although many educators focus on antibullying campaigns, creating a caring classroom goes to the heart of this problem. Students who can consider other kids' perspectives are less likely to bully than kids who cannot relate to other people. But it's not that simple. There are many reasons why students bully and engage in cruel behavior at school and online, and there's no simple solution that will make everyone get along. Many bullies stay outside the radar of teachers, tormenting their peers at opportune moments. Some bullies are popular and well-liked, drawing laughs and using ridicule to build their popularity. What can you do to stop bullying when it appears in your classroom? Here's an example of a bullying moment and how a teacher handles it:

John:	What's wrong with you? You're so ugly!
Jenny:	(no response)
John:	You're ugly.
Mr. Winter:	What are you doing, John?
John:	I'm not doing anything.
Mr. Winter:	What were you saying to Jenny?
John:	I was just talking.
Mr. Winter:	It didn't sound like talking to me.
John:	If it bothered her at all, she'd respond.
Mr. Winter:	This behavior isn't appropriate. I'm not going to tolerate this in my classroom.
John:	I was just kidding!
Mr. Winter:	John, this is not acceptable behavior—either inside or outside my class. I'd like to speak with you after class.
John:	This isn't going to hurt my grade, is it?

Within the context of this dialogue, John discovers that ridiculing a fellow student isn't acceptable. Mr. Winter makes a point of establishing ground rules for what is and isn't acceptable in his class.

This dialogue isn't going to solve the bullying problem entirely, but at least it sets a limit on what is and is not tolerated in the classroom.

Here's an example of building empathy into your schedule. We know that bullying goes on behind the scenes, but students aren't always aware that their actions can have devastating consequences. How can we teach students about these consequences? The best way to get students involved is to have them act out scenes in which bullying is stopped or prevented entirely. Students can write their own antibullying dialogues and share them with the larger group. Here is a dialogue that you can use as a starting point to launch a discussion about the importance of appreciating every student in your classroom:

Margie:	What's wrong with Susan?
Tara:	I don't see anything wrong with her.
Margie:	She keeps twisting her braid. And she talks weirdly. What is she, autistic?
Tara:	I don't think it matters if she acts a little different. She's a person, too, and we can try to be friends with her.
Margie:	I don't want to be friends with a weirdo.
Tara:	She may be fun to hang out with. We'll never know if you don't give her a chance. Why don't we go over and say hi right now?
Margie:	We can try.

In this dialogue, Margie points out that Susan has a mild form of autism. Margie looks at Susan from a distance, but Tara steers the conversation to friendly territory. This dialogue is critical because students with high-functioning autism are often more likely to be bullied in school than their peers. Very often these students are left out of group activities, parties, and other events.

Don't be afraid to use your imagination and memories to connect with the children you work with today.

Creating Dialogues

Students can write these kinds of dialogues and perform them in small groups. After showing a dialogue to students, place your class in small groups and assign students the following exercise:

> Write a dialogue featuring two or three people in which the participants learn about empathy and/or show empathy to each other. Then, perform your skit for the class. What did you learn from this activity?

You can also build empathy through creative activities. For example, your students can write and design a card for troops overseas. You can discuss how it would feel to be away from your family during the holidays. Kids will develop an appreciation for servicepeople who make the ultimate sacrifice for their country. This is a great activity because the cards that students send will have an immediate positive impact for both parties involved.

THINK LIKE A KID

As you create a caring classroom, don't forget what it feels like to be a kid. If you remember what it feels like to be 12 years old, you'll be more effective with seventh graders. If you recall what it felt like to go to school for the first time, you'll connect with kindergarten students. Don't be afraid to use your imagination and memories to connect with the children you work with today.

Imagine what it's like to be an only child for 10 years—and then to get a baby brother who takes away your parents' attention. Do you remember bringing money for a school lunch, expecting pizza but ending up with an egg salad sandwich instead? Do you remember what it feels like to be picked last for a sports team? Do you remember how you felt when you were the only person not invited to a birthday party?

As memories flow back, try to understand what your students are going through. How did you feel when someone reached out to you in a moment of need? You can make that kind of difference in a student's life today.

FINAL THOUGHTS

Creating an empathetic classroom is an ongoing process. You'll experience frustration, exhilaration, and skepticism. But even if you witness just one moment of empathy, you'll taste success. Embrace that moment and remember that your influence extends beyond the classroom.

DISCUSSION QUESTIONS

For Teachers

1. Which of the eight steps are you most excited to complete? Why?
2. Revisit the example dialogues shared in this chapter. How might you create these kinds of empathetic moments in your classroom?
3. How receptive have your students been to these ideas so far? Do you feel like you've made some progress?

For Students

1. In small groups, brainstorm three ways to create empathy within your classroom (e.g., more opportunities to talk to other students). Write down your ideas and be prepared to share with the class.
2. How can you demonstrate empathy to another student in your class this week?
3. How does generosity relate to empathy?

Chapter 3

How Can You Teach Empathy?

Empathy works so well because it does not require a solution. It requires only understanding.

—John Medina

As educators, we bring content knowledge and life experience to our classrooms. We want our students to perform well on standardized tests in comparison to children around the state and world. But our greatest joy is watching children grow and develop as people.

Sometimes empathy is lost in the shuffle. Empathy is difficult to teach because we encounter it at unexpected times. You can take students to a museum, but you can't guarantee they will experience the exhibits in the way you intended. Some students will find the paintings fascinating, while others will be bored. You can't see ahead of time what impact you will have outside the classroom.

In *With Love and Prayers: A Headmaster Speaks to the Next Generation*, Jarvis (2000) described receiving postcards from four different boys from Roxbury Latin School who were vacationing together in Florence. Two young men spent hours studying the works of Michelangelo and Botticelli, while another boy lamented the fact that Florence was hot during the summertime and filled with mosquitoes; the fourth boy commented on drinking in cafes. Jarvis wrote,

> These four Roxbury Latin graduates illustrate the different levels at which you can perceive the sensual world around you. Their perceptions are all accurate, but two of the four perceived and understood Florence at a far deeper and more profound level than the other two. They saw and perceived. They heard and understood. (pp. 38–39)

What can we learn from Jarvis's observation? Every student has a unique perspective on the world, a viewpoint that defines how much he appreciates empathy and other qualities. You cannot control where your students are coming from, but you can lead them on an exciting adventure that culminates in higher levels of empathy.

Teaching empathy is difficult, but that's why you are here—to do the difficult things. A robot can stand at the front of the classroom and present a prerecorded lecture. Students need a living, breathing person to make that lecture come alive beyond words on the page. When students learn in this authentic way, they become better people in every possible way. By teaching with empathy, you'll feel a deeper connection with your entire class.

EMBRACING SPONTANEOUS LEARNING

Teaching empathy is best done in a situational context. When you plan a lesson, you think about the content and core skills that students will acquire; empathy doesn't usually fall under a science, math, or reading lesson plan. Although you might find value in planning a lesson ahead of time, you can also address empathy in lessons in an unplanned way. Spontaneity adds to the power of the lecture.

You can't plan where every class session is heading. You can anticipate the kinds of questions students may ask, but you can't always see where the discussion is going. These unexpected questions allow you to tackle a subject in new ways. For instance, if your students ask questions about a current event, such as a family losing its home to a fire, you can discuss what it must feel like to lose your home and possessions. Then, your students can take action by raising funds through a bake sale to help this family in need. You've turned a question into a teaching moment about the power of empathy. This isn't something you can write into a lesson plan ahead of time; it has to come directly from you in the moment.

There's no foolproof way to insert empathy into a lesson because the best examples of empathy happen in unexpected ways. You can guide your students through difficult moments with sensitivity and grace. You can help students discover empathy within themselves.

Teaching empathy is difficult, but that's why you are here—to do the difficult things.

Still, although spontaneous moments of empathy and growth might be the ideal, as teachers, we plan our curriculum days in advance. We attend conferences during the summer where we buy curriculum to share with our students. We want our students to get critical information. The following section considers how we can plan some moments for empathy to flourish in the classroom.

ENHANCING CONTENT WITH CONNECTION

When you teach content, you share factual information with your students. Facts are important, but they don't motivate children like emotional experiences do. Textbooks provide information, but teachers can enhance these experiences with inspiration. For example, students can read a book about stars and understand their intricate qualities. But to give students an emotional experience, you can point out that stargazing is like time traveling; when you look at the night sky, you're looking at stars that no longer exist today.

Students can read about the 1980s or 1990s and watch television shows from that era, but you can tell them what it was like to attend elementary school when cell phones, texting, and e-mail were still developing. Students can study the Civil Rights Movement in a textbook, but you can bring this movement to life by inviting a participant from a march to speak before your class. Although your students won't have the chance to witness historical moments in "real time," you can bring history to life in your classroom. With imagination and creativity, your class will be an exciting place every day.

When you discuss the American pioneers heading west, it's an abstract concept to your students. You can make this moment come alive by showing pictures of wagons from that era, and then leading your students in a discussion about what it must have felt like to put all of your belongings in a wagon and head to a place you had never been before. History will come alive as your students "step in the footsteps" of pioneers as they explore this issue.

You can put a human touch on classroom experiences even when you can't leave the classroom. For instance, you might take a visual field trip of Monticello, Thomas Jefferson's home (visit https://www. monticello.org/exhibits-events/online-exhibits) or another notable location. With a few clicks of your finger, you can take your students on an exciting journey through history, mathematics, and astronomy. You don't need a huge budget or resources to do this, but you do need to think outside the box.

READING ABOUT EMPATHY

Many novels allow readers to examine empathy in action through different contexts. As we study empathy, students see how kindness and compassion make a difference in a variety of settings.

In Creech's (1994/2011) Newbery Award-winning novel, *Walk Two Moons*, Salamanca travels with her grandparents to the Midwest, where she hopes to find her biological mother. Sal (who is proud of her Native American heritage) discusses the importance of walking in someone's footsteps and states, "Don't judge a man until you have walked two moons in his moccasins" (p. 173). This novel raises an interesting question: In order to understand someone, do you have to experience exactly what she has?

Students know there are limits to feeling empathy for another person. Until we walk in another person's footsteps, we cannot truly understand his life. When Kayla was asked to write about expressing empathy toward another person, she stated:

> When my cousin was diagnosed with cancer, I had no idea how she felt. They told me she had to have her whole thyroid removed and that she could possibly lose her voice. When she came to me, she was overwhelmed. I did my best to empathize. I tried as hard as I could to be supportive and understanding of her pain and anguish. I let her know that although I could never fully understand what she was going through, she could use me as a support system. I tried to give her exactly what she needed to the best of my knowledge.

Kayla couldn't step into her cousin's mind. But she could support her cousin during this incredibly difficult time. Kayla's definition of empathy broadened to include being a supporting figure to a friend or relative in need.

Reading a novel is a good way for children to develop their own definition of empathy. For example, in E. B. White's *Charlotte's Web*, a spider spins words into her web to save the life of Wilbur, a pig. When people believe Wilbur can spell, he becomes a valued pig who will not be slaughtered. *Charlotte's Web* is a wonderful book to share with elementary-aged students, either by reading it aloud to the class or sharing it with advanced readers.

> **With imagination and creativity, your class will be an exciting place every day.**

You can also guide students to biographies of eminent people who demonstrated empathy in their careers. Students enjoy reading about the following:

- Nelson Mandela,
- Abraham Lincoln,
- Henry Ford,
- Emily Dickinson,
- Mother Theresa,
- Frank Boyden,
- Princess Diana,
- Clara Barton, and
- Jonas Salk.

These people made exceptional contributions to the world while demonstrating high levels of empathy. It's interesting to study their achievements through the prism of empathy rather than a more traditional approach. When we examine the lives of these eminent individuals, they follow the principles of President John F. Kennedy's inaugural address, "Ask not what your country can do for you; ask what you can do for your country." These individuals made great personal sacrifices to share their gifts and talents with humanity.

You can study a famous person's career path and see how concern for others affected that person's choices. Then, evaluate what constitutes an empathetic act—whether it is the giving of one's time or financial resources. There are also examples of empathetic individuals in films, television shows, and miniseries that your students might already be watching. Why not tap into student interests when teaching empathy? Figure 3 includes a list of movies and books that promote empathy.

WRITING ABOUT EMPATHY

Many students feel more comfortable writing about empathy than discussing it. When these children open up about their experiences, you can feel their emotions flow from the page. But it's not always easy for kids to open up. Writing allows students the opportunity to process an experience and to think about it deeply.

When Otto Frank first read his daughter Anne's diary, he was surprised at the intensity of her feelings (Noonan, 2011). He had talked to her every day for 14 years, but he'd never known his daughter's level of empathy. Frank later said, "For me, it was a revelation. There was a completely different Anne to the child I had lost. I had no idea of the depth of her thoughts and feelings" (para. 3).

Keep an open mind and make your classroom a safe zone where students can be their true selves.

Movies
Beauty and the Beast (1991, 2017)
The Breakfast Club (1985)
Bridge to Terabithia (2007)
Bully (2001)
The Chronicles of Narnia: The Lion, the Witch and the Wardrobe (2005)
E.T. the Extra-Terrestrial (1982)
Freaky Friday (2003)
Harry Potter and the Sorcerer's Stone (2001)
Green Book (2018)
A Little Princess (1995)
Pollyanna (1960)
To Kill a Mockingbird (1962)

Books
The Best-Loved Doll by Rebecca Caudill
The Great Gatsby by F. Scott Fitzgerald
Leo the Late Bloomer by Robert Kraus
The Lion, the Witch and the Wardrobe by C. S. Lewis
The One and Only Ivan by Katherine Applegate
The Other Half of Life by Kim Ablon Whitney
Our Town: A Play in Three Acts by Thornton Wilder
Out of Dust by Karen Hesse
A Single Shard by Linda Sue Park
Sounder by William H. Armstrong
Tuck Everlasting by Natalie Babbitt
Where the Red Fern Grows by Wilson Rawls
Where the Sidewalk Ends by Shel Silverstein
Winters With the Pelicans: A Basketball Memoir by Walter Rabetz
The Witch of Blackbird Pond by Elizabeth George Speare
The Wonderful Wizard of Oz by L. Frank Baum
To Kill a Mockingbird by Harper Lee

Figure 3. Movies and books that promote empathy.

Like Frank Otto, every day we work with students who see the world with intense thoughts and feelings. When we allow our students to write about empathy, we see the kaleidoscope of their feelings on the page. As teachers, we are capable of feeling deeply, of being haunted by moments when we could have done more, and of growing to a greater level of understanding. As we read student responses, we find deep emotions between the lines. These thoughts and feelings may never come out in a class discussion. It's important to keep an open mind and to allow our students to express empathy in new and dynamic ways. Sometimes we have to put ourselves on the line for our classes.

What does it feel like to put ourselves on the line? In a column in *The Washington Post*, Patti Davis (2018), daughter of Ronald and Nancy Reagan, wrote a poignant reflection about the late George H. W. Bush's eulogy for Ronald Reagan in 2004. Davis wrote,

> The tears he fought against brought my family and me to tears. It was one of those moments when you know that the person who is speaking is stripping his soul bare and letting you in. I wish now we had told him how deeply his eulogy moved us. We talked about it on the long flight back across the country to California, where my father would be buried and our time of private mourning would begin. It came up often—that moment when Bush's voice cracked, when tears intruded upon his words, when he was raw and honest in how much his heart was hurting. (para. 2–3)

When we think back on our teaching careers, these moments of vulnerability and openness will stay with us forever. As Hilary Cooper once said, "Life is not measured by the number of breaths we take, but by the moments that take our breath away." None of these moments can be rehearsed or planned ahead of time; we have to let them happen.

Let empathy grow in your classroom, but don't plan every moment. You can't predict the emotional responses that people will have, nor can you anticipate how your students will react to material. Keep an open mind and make your classroom a safe zone where students can be their true selves.

ASSESSING AND GRADING EMPATHY

Empathy can't be graded on a traditional rubric. It's difficult to grade this quality on a test, paper, or in a classroom situation, as we tend to reward students the most points for the "right" answer. Let's think about how we would grade empathy if we had to.

Would we grade empathy through student interactions? It's difficult to assess the full nature of interactions in a classroom, just as it is in real life. Two people may appear to be friends based on friendly interactions. But the true test of that friendship comes down to whether they "have each other's back" in a difficult situation. These friendships play out over the course of years, not days. In a classroom, we see only a microcosm of friendships. We can't assess whether students are just being friendly toward each other or whether empathy exists beneath the surface until they are placed in a difficult situation.

Can we grade empathy on a paper? Sometimes it's easiest to see empathy within a journal entry or paper. At one point I asked my students to write about a moment when they chose to act with empathy and what they learned from the experience. Reading through my students' journal entries, I saw a deeper version of every person than I knew in real life. But the level of empathy expressed depended on the situation and how deeply they engaged with this writing prompt.

Traditional rubrics focus on spelling, grammar, organization of thoughts, the structure of a paper, and the flow of the piece. None of these categories relate directly to empathy, which is a more elusive quality to grade. To put empathy into a rubric, we would require that empathy appear in students' papers instead of allowing it to grow holistically. Requiring students to write about empathy could take away from their natural train of thought. Empathy is most powerful when it's naturally demonstrated in a spontaneous situation.

Can we grade empathy on tests? We would be grading students based on what they *think* they would do in a difficult situation—and not what they have done. In a history class, students may write about how they would act during the Holocaust, yet they will never have the opportunity to demonstrate this heroism in real life. In essays, students reason through situations in the way they expect that their teachers would want. We don't get a full understanding of how students would act in a real-life situation based upon their test responses or papers. Empathy remains a very elusive—if not impossible—quality to grade in a test situation.

We can't grade empathy like spelling or grammar. We can't say that a student who claims that she would offer half her food to a refugee is less empathetic than someone who would give the shirt off her back to a stranger. But if we can't use a traditional rubric for empathy, this raises the question of whether we can assess it at all. How can you teach something that you can't grade? How can you incentivize students to become more empathetic toward each other if you can't assess their improvement and reward it accordingly? And how can we grade a quality that takes years to develop?

This leads us back to the difficult truth: Some students will gain little besides a dictionary understanding of empathy, while other students will become deeper and more reflective human beings. We can't predict where our lessons will take our students, because our students have qualities that we cannot see and understand. Perhaps the best way to bring empathy into grading is indirectly. We can write open-ended questions on essay exams and journal entries that lead to the possibility of empathetic expressions in response.

How do you teach empathy, knowing each student will get something different out of your lesson? When students develop an emotional connection to a lesson, they are far more likely to get something out of it. If students meet a Holocaust survivor, they will feel a stronger connection to people who survived the tragedies of World War II. When your class discusses early childhood mortality in the 18th century, you can visit an old cemetery and make artistic rubbings of the headstones there. When you personalize a lesson, students develop a connection to distant events and realize that people in an earlier era weren't that different from themselves. That is the beginning of empathy.

Teaching empathy is complex, but each student has a unique experience in your class every single day. You cannot universalize what students get out of a mathematics lesson, nor can you guarantee that every child will internalize the same message in a lesson linked to empathy. Some students will benefit more from the lesson than others. However, you can encourage empathy to become a natural part of your students' lives.

FINAL THOUGHTS

Teaching empathy is difficult, but you can handle this challenge. Whether you have been teaching for months or decades, you have impacted countless students. By implementing the activities and exercises in this book, you'll achieve great success. You may not see benefits from your efforts initially. But no matter what happens, keep the faith—you are doing a lot of great things!

DISCUSSION QUESTIONS

For Teachers

1. How can you create authentic lessons that incorporate op-portunities for empathy?
2. What novels or films could you use in the classroom to deep-en students' understanding of empathy?
3. How will you assess students' levels of empathy in your class-room?

For Students

1. What have you learned about empathy so far? Has anything surprised you?
2. How can you teach empathy to a younger child?
3. Think about your favorite books or movies. What characters demonstrate empathy, and how?

Chapter 4

How Does Emotional Intelligence Relate to Empathy?

In a very real sense we have two minds, one that thinks and one that feels.

—Daniel Goleman

Whether you are a new teacher or a seasoned educator, you've heard of emotional intelligence. Usually we focus on teaching our students curriculum and preparing them for tests. We spend so much time teaching reading, writing, and arithmetic skills that we don't have time (or energy) to worry about children's emotional intelligence. But this focus may be doing a disservice to our students.

Do people need high levels of emotional intelligence to develop authentic connections with each other? How is empathy connected to emotional intelligence? You may have encountered the concept of emotional intelligence before in school or in your teaching career. This chapter will help you understand this concept, as well as its relation to empathy, more deeply.

HISTORY OF EMOTIONAL INTELLIGENCE

The term *emotional intelligence* dates back to the 1960s. Many people haven't studied emotional intelligence, and their knowledge of it comes from media sources and news headlines. Emotional intelligence is a newer idea, but it gained traction quickly. When you mention this term to friends and colleagues, chances are they've at least heard of it.

In 1964, Beldoch used the term *emotional intelligence* for the first time in a paper. Emotional intelligence was then referenced several times during the next 30 years. Mayer and Salovey (1993) first defined the term in the way we think of it today. But the publication of Goleman's (1995) best-selling book *Emotional Intelligence* brought this term to millions of people. Goleman wrote,

> Two fundamentally different ways of knowing interact to construct our mental life. One, the rational mind, is the mode of comprehension we are typically conscious of: more prominent in awareness, thoughtful, able to power and reflect. But alongside that there is another system of knowing: impulsive and powerful, if sometimes illogical—the emotional mind. (p. 8)

Emotional intelligence (EI) is a deep understanding of our own emotions and how our actions impact other people. Goleman included the categories of self-awareness, self-regulation, motivation, empathy, and social skills under emotional intelligence.

WHY TEACH EMOTIONAL INTELLIGENCE?

Emotional intelligence can't be seen on the surface; we know it when we see it demonstrated, but it's difficult to quantify. It isn't something a person automatically acquires with age and experience. This raises critical questions:

- Can emotional intelligence be taught?
- Can we teach students kindness?
- Can we educate students' emotions along with their minds?
- Should we teach emotional intelligence along with other curriculum initiatives?

Emotional intelligence is a deep understanding of our own emotions and how our actions impact other people.

Teachers are trained to develop syllabi and lesson plans that connect to standardized tests, not to teach emotional or moral growth. We appreciate caring students, but we don't award extra points for sharing notes with a classmate, tutoring at a writing center, or peer editing a friend's paper. However, students with high levels of emotional intelligence benefit by connecting with peers at a deeper level than those who think from one perspective. They can read a Shakespearean play with a greater attention to what it says about human nature. They can develop a new theory in a psychology class that might become the basis for a senior thesis. They can create an educational study that will change the way we see the world.

Emotional intelligence is also critical for students' future careers. Emotional intelligence helps people in the workplace, influencing their job performance and even leadership skills. According to Goleman (1995),

> Today companies worldwide routinely look through the lens of EI in hiring, promoting, and developing their employees. For instance, Johnson and Johnson . . . found that in divisions around the world, those identified at midcareer as having high leadership potential were stronger in EI competencies than were their less promising peers. (p. 6)

Goleman concluded that emotional intelligence affects career success because it can help a person with a great skill set move into a higher level of expertise. A doctor who understands medicine will perform well in the operating room, but understanding human nature will help her connect well with her patients. A school administrator with leadership skills can give an effective lecture, but his emotional intelligence will help him develop a genuine connection with hundreds of students. A teacher who works with the curriculum will teach her students content knowledge; her understanding of the human psyche will inspire the development of emotional intelligence in her students. Emotional intelligence takes a person from good to great, from mediocrity to excellence.

Goleman's (1995) emotional intelligence theory states that people have two minds—one that thinks and one that feels. If we teach to the thinking mind, we end up with logical, rational outcomes. But there's something missing—that emotional touch, which adds a special flavor to life. Do we want our students to be so rational that they never feel anything?

The truth is that we have so many other things to worry about that emotional intelligence falls by the wayside. Did our students perform well on standardized tests? Can they progress to the next grade? We worry about students whose parents can't send lunch money and about children whose parents are getting divorced. We don't often analyze soft data, like emotional intelligence and empathy. In fairness, we don't consciously make the decision not to teach emotional intelligence strategies; we run out of time.

Emotional intelligence takes a person from good to great, from mediocrity to excellence.

HOW DOES EMPATHY RELATE TO EMOTIONAL INTELLIGENCE?

Goleman (1995) described empathy as a category of emotional intelligence; a caring person is someone who understands the feelings and needs of other people. Having emotional intelligence helps us understand another person's perspective, feelings, and thoughts.

Empathy is a facet of emotional intelligence, which pertains to the overall ability to understand another person's feelings and life experiences. When we consider emotional intelligence as broad concept, it's important to look back at Goleman's (1995) definition, which includes several categories of emotional intelligence: self-awareness, self-regulation, motivation, empathy, and social skills. A good way to teach these concepts is to have students develop a web of ideas that are central to emotional intelligence, as shown in Figure 4.

For younger students, these concepts may be difficult to understand if you teach them all at once. In my modified web of emotional intelligences (see Figure 5), I have included the concepts of resilience, sympathy, compassion, empathy, and kindness, which might fall under its umbrella. Empathy is an important concept within emotional intelligence; a person with a high level of emotional intelligence has empathy, sympathy, and the ability to understand human nature. Young children may enjoy developing their own webs about emotional intelligence with terms that they have brainstormed during class

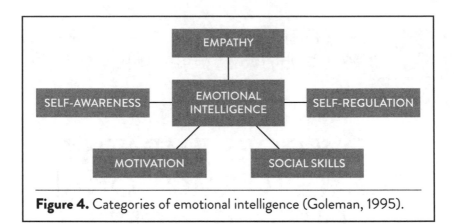

Figure 4. Categories of emotional intelligence (Goleman, 1995).

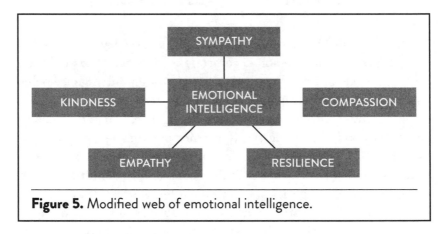

Figure 5. Modified web of emotional intelligence.

discussions. Student-friendly definitions for these terms include the following:

- **Sympathy:** Feeling pity for another person's misfortune.
- **Empathy:** The ability to understand the feelings of another person.
- **Kindness:** Being friendly, generous, or considerate.
- **Compassion:** Sympathetic concern for the misfortune of another.
- **Resilience:** Toughness; the ability to spring back quickly.

When we teach students about emotional intelligence, it's far more effective to break down the concept into qualities like empathy, resilience, and compassion. Breaking emotional intelligence into separate categories makes it manageable. If we taught every component of emotional intelligence at once, our students would be overwhelmed. This book focuses on empathy as a concept to teach within the larger umbrella. Teaching empathy fits neatly into the idea of teaching emotional intelligence in a school setting.

Think of it this way: We don't teach science as a broad course to high school and college students; we focus on specific areas like chemistry, biology, and physics. So it makes sense to teach empathy, compassion, and other qualities that belong under the general emotional intelligence category rather than trying to teach everything at once.

When students feel comfortable with empathy, you can develop a conceptual map (see Figure 5) of other qualities that fall under the emotional intelligence umbrella, including sympathy, compassion, resilience, kindness, etc. You can create a map and explain how these concepts contribute to emotional intelligence. Students find this exercise interesting because it allows them to study empathy along with other important qualities that constitute emotional intelligence.

Developing emotional intelligence is a lifelong process.

You can discuss whether or not all of these qualities constitute emotional intelligence, and if students would like to add more categories. Students will see a relationship between emotional intelligence and these other qualities. Alternatively, you may use the original concept map (see Figure 4) derived around Goleman's (1995) definition of emotional intelligence and explain these different concepts to students.

Some of the categories related to emotional intelligence are already being cultivated in preschool and kindergarten. In *All I Really Needed to Know I Learned in Kindergarten*, Fulghum (2004) described the importance of sharing and caring—skills that students learn in kindergarten and carry throughout their lives. Many of the qualities that children develop in kindergarten will help them become caring and compassionate people later on. Kindergarten is a wonderful time to develop a relationship with peers, a sense of self, and qualities of character.

Developing emotional intelligence is a lifelong process, but it's exciting to watch your students take the first steps along the way. Emotional intelligence is not necessarily attained in a chronological fashion; it can take years of experience and hardship to feel a greater connection with other people.

FINAL THOUGHTS

As you work with your class, you'll discover that emotional intelligence and empathy are closely linked. As a broad concept, emotional intelligence includes empathy, compassion, sympathy, kindness, and resilience. Empathy is a wonderful concept to teach, and it can lead to a greater level of emotional intelligence among your students.

DISCUSSION QUESTIONS

For Teachers

1. Reflect on the relationship between emotional intelligence and empathy. How are these two concepts linked together?
2. As an educator, when did you become aware of the importance of emotional intelligence? Did you study it in school, or did you learn about it through popular culture?
3. How has your definition of general intelligence changed with your understanding of emotional intelligence? How important is emotional intelligence in a school setting?

For Students

1. What qualities make a person emotionally intelligent?
2. How does an emotionally intelligent person behave? Do you know a person like this?
3. Can you increase your emotional intelligence? How would you do this?

Chapter 5

How Can You Maintain Empathy in Your Classroom?

> I believe empathy is the most essential quality of civilization.
>
> —Roger Ebert

During the first week of class, students are open to meeting new people. But as the year progresses, children move into smaller groups and cliques. Students become immersed in afterschool activities, clubs, and finding their way through academia. Sometimes empathy gets lost in the shuffle. How do you maintain empathy in your classroom?

MIDYEAR ICEBREAKERS

Although icebreakers work well at the beginning of the year, there are limitations to these kinds of activities. Jamie, a student in my class, wrote about empathy and the limitations of icebreakers:

Empathy is vital to human interaction and to improving the overall quality of life. Empathy is something that needs to be discussed more in a school setting. At the beginning of the semester we do class activities like icebreakers to get to know each other. After the "getting to know you" time ends, we don't really talk to each other again, unless we are working on group projects. You can spend a whole semester sitting next to someone and not even know her name. So we must continue icebreaker activities throughout the semester.

When the icebreaker activities end, it is critical that students continue to develop empathy.

Instead of using icebreaker activities once a year, consider incorporating group work into other class activities or doing icebreakers in a slightly different format. Figure 6 is an example of a follow-up icebreaker to give students when they return from winter break.

With a follow-up icebreaker activity, students will meet new people as the year progresses. When students know a wider group of people, they are more likely to demonstrate empathy. Students may have developed their circle of friends, but this activity gives students the opportunity to meet people while working on a low-stress activity. Students will enjoy taking a break and developing further connections during this class period. Some of these connections may turn into lifelong friendships.

GROUP ACTIVITIES

Another way to continue growing empathy is to introduce activities that engage the intellectual interest of students. One activity that I have created is to have students work in small groups to create

---

Find someone in class whom you don't know very well. Ask each other the following questions:
- What did you do over winter break?
- What was the best part of winter break?
- What was the worst part of winter break?
- Are you excited to be back in school?

Be prepared to introduce your new friend to the rest of the class!

Figure 6. Winter break follow-up icebreaker.

---

futuristic toys (see Figure 7). Kids become so focused on this activity that they don't realize they are developing creativity and presentation skills in the process. If you break students into new groups ahead of time, they'll also make new friends in the process.

Figure 8 is another example of a group activity that you can share with your students. This activity allows students to develop social skills, public speaking skills, and new connections all at the same time. Students love making predictions about whether Facebook will have a three-dimensional component and if cell phones will be holographic. This is a great way to reestablish connections throughout the year and to create a friendly environment that will hopefully last for the rest of the year.

How else can you maintain this friendly atmosphere as the year progresses? Some teachers mix students into groups randomly so that students are always meeting new people. Other teachers place students in groups for the year, believing core groups increase cohesiveness within the classroom. You have the potential to grow empathy in your classroom all year long. With your attention and efforts, empathy can become a way of life in your classroom.

The year is 2035. You work in a toy and game design company as a creative designer. What toy will you create? You can create a three-dimensional game set, a vanishing doll, or whatever comes to your imagination. You will work in small groups.

- Start by drawing a picture of your toy or game.
- Then, write down details and selling points (Why should kids buy your game?).
- Lastly, prepare to share your idea with the class. Remember, you'll want to promote your game with a great sales pitch!

Figure 7. Futuristic toys activity.

With your group, begin brainstorming ideas for what technology will be like in 2050. Think about today's technologies (smartphones, Facebook, etc.) and how they will evolve and change during the next 20–30 years.

- First, draw a picture of some of this new technology.
- Next, think about how you will present your ideas to the class. Make sure everyone in your group has a speaking role.
- Present your ideas to the class.

Figure 8. Technology in 2050 activity.

REVISING DEFINITIONS OF EMPATHY

How can you make sure that empathy isn't just another assignment? Each time students use empathy, they change their approach to the concept in subtle ways. Empathy isn't just a vocabulary word; it's a living concept. When students develop a connection to empathy, they will live it in their own lives.

As part of your work in maintaining empathy in the classroom, have your students revisit their personal definitions of empathy. Many students will redefine empathy in subtle ways as they experience it. Students can respond to the following prompt:

> How has your definition of empathy changed based on your experiences in this class? Revisit your first definition of empathy to determine how you should modify it based on recent experiences. Then, write a new definition of empathy. Explain how your perception of this word has altered.

As your students redefine empathy through their own words and experiences, it will become more significant in their lives. They will internalize empathy and use it in exciting ways. You'll see empathy flourish in contexts you never would have predicted.

To nurture empathy, assign follow-up exercises. An open-ended assignment in which students write about empathy could be an effective exercise, particularly if students discuss observations of empathy in their lives. Such prompts include the following:

- Empathy is just another word in the dictionary until we bring it to life in our lives. Write about a moment when you brought empathy to life.
- Consider the following quote: "A book is a block of paper until you open it and begin reading." How does this relate to empathy and relationships?

These statements result in interesting and dynamic responses. Children will see empathy in their own lives and write about it in compelling ways.

Empathy isn't just a vocabulary word; it's a living concept.

Every class has a different dynamic. What works in one class may not work in another, so use your best judgment with these activities. You can modify these exercises to suit the needs of your class. Do what works best for the children you work with.

LEARN ABOUT EMPATHY FROM YOUR STUDENTS

Students have a great deal to teach us. Six hundred years ago, Chaucer wrote, "Gladly would he learn and gladly teach." If we keep an open mind, we can learn just as much from our students as they learn from us. Every student who comes into our classroom has something different to teach us about life. What can we teach students about empathy, and what can we learn from them in return?

During my time as an educator, my students have taught me more than I have taught them. Every student has a unique life story and experiences. Every student expresses creative and innovative thoughts. Even students who claim that they don't have an ounce of creativity can imagine and create amazing things. My students have taught me about empathy in ways I never could have imagined.

Early in my teaching career, I watched students help each other during peer editing. In my advanced fiction class, one student wrote professional-level critiques. Another student befriended a girl who was legally blind, and the girls worked together on group projects. Several students befriended and included a young man with disabilities in their group. My students demonstrated kindness and understanding toward each other in a way that made teaching a joyful experience.

Empathy is far more powerful when it comes from students than when it is choreographed by a teacher or administrator. For example, at Marjory Stoneman Douglas High School, students organized a nationwide event, March for Our Lives, after their school suffered a major shooting in February 2018. This movement was led by students and included people from all walks of life.

If we encourage students to share their life experiences with us, we're sending a powerful message: *You have value, and your definition of empathy matters*. Never forget that your students have the power to change the world. When students take charge, we send a strong message: *Your ability to make decisions matters. We are here for you always, but you can make an impact without our guidance*. When we stand on the sidelines, we are sending a very powerful message about our confidence in young people in general.

This leads to a greater question: Do we need to learn more about empathy ourselves? To fully understand empathy, we must see the world from different viewpoints. We must develop compassion and understanding for the people in our own lives. In order to *teach* empathy, we must *live* empathy.

How can we become more empathetic? When we step outside of our comfort zones, we develop higher levels of empathy. Giving money and time to a charitable organization increases empathy. Volunteering at a homeless shelter is also a way to develop empathy. Creating connections with people outside of your immediate social scene can be an excellent way to develop this skill.

> **If we encourage students to share their life experiences with us, we're sending a powerful message: *You have value, and your definition of empathy matters.***

Have you met new people lately? Think about the organizations you are involved with and whether you are truly welcoming to outsiders. Most adults do not think that they are in cliques. But chances are you're in a group that has some exclusivity. Instead of sitting at your table with the same group you have been part of for many years, invite a new person to lunch. When you open a door, you're building bridges with new people. That may be the greatest act of empathy of all.

TAKING EMPATHY TO THE NEXT LEVEL

Every time we step into our classrooms, we redefine empathy. Although empathy can happen spontaneously, you can grow empathy on a regular basis. Empathy must be nurtured and encouraged within your classroom every day. Empathy takes a new direction each time it is implemented by your students. Some children exhibit this trait in dynamic ways, while others express empathy in more predictable ways. Let your students express empathy in a manner that is suitable to their personalities and beneficial to their peers.

As a teacher, you'll see students take this concept to the next level. Some children will volunteer at pet shelters. Other kids will write holiday cards to men and women serving overseas. Many children will volunteer with the Special Olympics. Kids will see opportunities to develop empathy in their own school, and they'll reach out to people they've never been friends with before. Empathy can occur on a large or small canvas, and there are plenty of exciting opportunities every day to make this happen.

No matter what path empathy takes, it's exciting to see students implementing empathy in their lives. As teachers, what more could we ask for?

THE DANGER OF TOO MUCH EMPATHY

Is there such a thing as too much empathy? Will your students be negatively affected if you overuse this concept? Let's think back to the heyday of the self-esteem movement, which flourished in the 1980s and 1990s. Every child received a trophy at every event; there were no "winners" or "losers" because every child's performance was celebrated. This movement had noble intentions. Having self-esteem is a positive thing. But there were some drawbacks of this movement that didn't manifest until years later.

> **When you make an activity mandatory, students think about the *least* they can do to accomplish the requirement. When an activity is voluntary, students think about the *most* they can do to make an impact.**

I have a perfect attendance award from that era for ballet classes, which is somewhere in in the basement of my parents' house. My mother scoffed at this trophy for perfect attendance when I had actually missed two sessions! Whether you grew up in the self-esteem era or raised a child in that time period, you probably have a participation trophy gathering dust in your basement, too. Many years later, these awards still do not represent achievement, accomplishment, or effort; they just reward showing up.

We don't want empathy to turn into another self-esteem movement, but we do want this concept to grow within our classrooms and communities. Let's spread empathy, but not at the expense of other subjects and skills that we're required to teach.

Will the empathy movement cause a backlash? Possibly. It's beneficial to bring empathy into your classroom, but don't drown your students in this idea. Encourage children to mingle outside their crowd, but don't force connections. Children may resent giving valentines or party invites to everyone in the class if it is required; it's better to encourage outreach opportunities. When you make an activity mandatory, students think about the *least* they can do to accomplish the requirement. When an activity is voluntary, students think about the *most* they can do to make an impact.

If empathy is implemented frequently (rather than naturally infused into the curriculum) it can be detrimental. If every lesson plan includes empathy, students will roll their eyes and say, "Not again!" Everything should be done in moderation. If you bring empathy up at regular intervals, it will be more effective than if you discuss it every day. Less is more. It's best to infuse empathy naturally into your curriculum and to have faith that your students will bring concern into their daily lives.

YOUR STUDENTS ARE WORKS IN PROGRESS

No matter how old you are, you are a work in progress. Every day you learn new things, meet new people, and enjoy fresh experiences. When you watch a sunset today, it will be a different experience than it was yesterday. We are growing and changing every day of our lives, and our students are exhibiting even faster rates of growth. A student who acts immaturely today may surprise us tomorrow. When we consider life as a continuum, our students are at the earliest stages of development. Whether you work with first graders or high school seniors, your students have a great deal of maturing to do.

Most teenagers' brains are immature even at the end of high school (Jensen & Nutt, 2015), so don't expect them to act with concern for others in all situations. If you're fortunate, you'll witness incredible growth and development over the course of the year. But even the most mature 17-year-old will continue to experience growth and development later in life.

Every day is an opportunity to grow and change in countless ways. Just because you're an adult doesn't prevent you from participating in this exciting process. You are a work-in-progress, too! Savor those moments when you feel growth and internal development within yourself. Then, witness this exciting growth in your students.

SELF-ACTUALIZATION

Your students have tremendous talents in school, sports, and social activities. We must always look beyond IQ scores. We aren't just teaching students; we're working with future citizens of the world. When students think beyond self-interest, they demonstrate empathy in new and compelling ways.

> **Development is invisible on the surface, but inside it's momentous. Students are having life-changing experiences in your class, even if you can't see it.**

When we think about Maslow's (1943/2013) hierarchy of needs, many people are successful at the early levels. Hopefully your students have their basic needs attended to, including sleep, water, nutrition, safety, and loving people in their lives. They may have developed esteem, which is an upper level in the Maslow hierarchy, and they may feel good about themselves.

Self-actualization is at the top of the Maslow (1943/2013) hierarchy, and it's far more difficult to achieve. Self-actualization includes morality, creativity, problem solving, and a lack of prejudice. To become a self-actualized person is very difficult, and most people never make it to this level. That's why empathy is so important. Showing empathy toward another person requires morality, creativity, problem solving, and a lack of prejudice. Students who exhibit empathy are taking the first steps toward self-actualization. To become a self-actualized person represents the highest level in the Maslow hierarchy. If your students demonstrate empathy toward each other, they will make great contributions to society.

Becoming self-actualized requires feeling genuine concern for someone else. There's no time frame for when this could occur. It could happen to a first grader or to a 90-year-old. If you are lucky, you'll witness children taking the first steps toward self-actualization in your classroom. Whether you work with gifted, general, or special education doesn't matter. Everyone has the capacity to feel concern for his or her peers.

Depending upon what happens in your classroom, you'll witness different outcomes. Some kids will have defining moments, while others will appear unchanged at the end of the year. Development is invisible on the surface, but inside it's momentous. Students are having life-changing experiences in your class, even if you can't see it.

DEVELOPING AN EMPATHETIC IDENTITY

Students are rewarded for performing well on tests and creating high-level products. Many talented students feel tremendous pressure to perform academically. It's not uncommon for class rankings to be determined to the hundredth of a point. Students must attain high grade point averages and SAT or ACT scores to ensure they will be accepted at elite colleges.

Given this competitive environment, do students have time to express empathy toward each other? Some high schools require community service, which allows students to develop empathy as part of an extracurricular activity. Students engage in a daily grind, participating in multiple extracurricular activities, studying for tests, and working a part-time job. Kids don't receive extra points because they helped a classmate prepare for an exam, nor do they get a lift in their class rank because they volunteered at a Special Olympics swimming competition.

Students have a responsibility to nurture their own gifts, but there's always time to help others, too. Community service is an emotional maturation process, not a graduation requirement. When students help other people, they experience intrinsic rewards that cannot be measured by grade point average or class ranking. Empathy becomes a natural and holistic part of these students' identities.

TALENT DEVELOPMENT

Every student has the potential to develop empathy, but it's more difficult to reach some students than others. Because you're dealing with many kinds of personalities, it's difficult to nurture your entire class at once. Understanding how students develop their talents is a good starting point for understanding how to help them develop empathy.

Becoming a caring person takes years, not days. In *Developing Talent in Young People*, Bloom (1985) described three significant stages of talent development that young people go through. At the first stage, children are exposed to an activity in a fun and playful way. At the second stage, children demonstrate interest in this activity and receive sustained training and support from coaches or teachers. At the third stage, children work toward becoming world-class performers in their field of interest. To become a world-class performer in any field takes years of training and dedication.

How does Bloom's (1985) theory of talent development relate to your students? Your students are at the earliest stages of developing empathy. Students don't attend empathy practice in the same way that they would go to soccer practice. So how can they practice empathy? Should they volunteer at a soup kitchen or donate to a charity? Or should empathy be more integral to their lives? If we can't think of a way to develop empathy in a progressive manner, it's unfair to expect our students to attain high levels of it upon entering our class. The important thing to remember is that your students have the capacity to develop empathy to a higher level this year.

How does a student progress toward a higher level of empathy? Using Bloom's (1985) model, students can develop high levels of empathy even by the end of high school. While studying at The Loomis Chaffee School (2019) in Windsor, CT, Beatrice Dang developed a high level of empathy. During her senior project, Dang interviewed eight war veterans for her book *Those Who Served: A Collection of Interviews With Military Veterans*. She gave a presentation about her project to the local community and presented copies of her published book to the veterans who were interviewed. Dang donated the remaining funds raised from book sales to the Wounded Warriors Fund. During this experience, Dang developed empathy at several levels—from being able to ask compelling questions to sharing her story with the community.

We can't expect all students to have high levels of empathy, but we can help children grow into better people. Just like we wouldn't expect a child to write a Pulitzer Prize-winning novel, we can't expect students to demonstrate concern for others at the same level as Abraham Lincoln or Mother Theresa. Becoming a caring person takes years of practice, just like other talents do. Because it's hard to define what "practicing" empathy means, this complicates the process.

Developing empathy takes as much practice as any other activity. With a sport, we can evaluate a student's progress based on statistics and other data, but developing empathy is a slower and more circuitous process. Although the media highlights stories of children whose volunteer projects become national drives, most children develop empathy at a slower rate or on a smaller scale. It takes life experiences to become truly interested in other people, and it takes a lifetime to develop empathy. Your students can begin this exciting process today.

FINAL THOUGHTS

If you see empathy as a journey (and not a final destination), you'll witness special moments in your classroom every day. Your students will take this concept in new and exciting directions as the school year progresses.

Empathy doesn't follow a linear path. Your students may be considerate one day but misbehave the following afternoon. No one action that we take today will directly translate into a caring classroom tomorrow. The best way to maintain empathy is to infuse it into your curriculum and life. No matter what happens, don't get discouraged. Keep growing empathy in your classroom, and your students will surprise you behind the scenes.

DISCUSSION QUESTIONS

For Teachers

1. How can you maintain empathy in your classroom? After trying different approaches, what works best for your students?
2. How can you help your students develop higher levels of empathy during the course of the school year?
3. Are there drawbacks to promoting empathy in your classroom?

For Students

1. In small groups, brainstorm ideas for how you can grow and maintain empathy. Share your ideas with the entire class.
2. Write a short paragraph about the challenges of maintaining empathy in a classroom.
3. What does it mean to be a work in progress?

Chapter 6

How Can Students Give Back to Society?

> To whom much is given, much is required.
> —John F. Kennedy

These days, kids are busier than in previous generations, and their hectic lifestyles begin in elementary school. By the time they hit high school, your students have classes, on-campus activities, jobs, and sports. How can students add another activity to their overfilled lives? Does empathy really have a place in the educational experiences of students, or should kids focus on academic achievements?

Here's the good news: Every day kids are making a difference in the world in multiple contexts. There are many ways to contribute to the world. Your students will feel a confidence boost when they help others in need. It's never too early to develop empathy. Your students don't have to graduate from high school to be caring people. With the presence of GoFundMe pages and other resources, children can develop meaningful projects even while in elementary school. With your guidance, students can begin their journey toward empathy today.

THE EMPATHY CONNECTION

Empathy is a critical quality for *all* students. Some students gravitate naturally toward empathy, but others must be taught this concept. In order to appreciate empathy, students must experience it directly. If students have never experienced empathy, they will have difficulty expressing concern for others.

> **We can't always tell students how to act or what to do, but we can give them confidence in their own decision making.**

How can we teach students to act with empathy? The best way to do this is to share the concept of empathy, and then watch how students apply in specific situations. At my mother's wake on August 22, 2018, my childhood babysitter, Amy, told me a story. When Amy gave birth to a child with special needs, she approached my mother for advice. My mother was the parent of a child with Down syndrome, and she always helped those who came to her with questions. (A video featuring my mother's work with Brian, "Finding Miracles," is available at https://www.youtube.com/watch?v=xC4e9-N7rXE.)

When Amy's son was born, she wasn't sure how to explain his disabilities to her older child. "How will I tell Cody?" Amy asked. "How will he understand?"

My mother answered, "When the moment arrives, *you will know what to say.*"

With this powerful statement, my mother gave Amy confidence in her ability as a parent and the ultimate compliment: *You will know what to do in that moment.* My mother gave Amy an important gift: an expression of confidence in her parenting abilities in a difficult situation.

The greatest gift we can offer students is to have faith in their expressions of empathy. We can't always tell students how to act or what to do, but we can give them confidence in their own decision making.

The world is filled with shades of gray. In many situations, there are no clear-cut answers for how to behave. You can talk about empathy all day long, but what really matters is how you act in that moment. Talk is cheap, but actions take effort, planning, and thinking. We see this all of the time in real-life situations. Many people volunteer for an organization once or twice, but some people put years into a project and make a huge impact.

It doesn't take expertise to develop empathy. You just have to stretch outside yourself and consider how another person feels and thinks. Then you must take action and bring positive change to the world. Sometimes, though, it's difficult to act with empathy. Although it may be easy to hold a door open for the person behind you, expressing empathy in more challenging situations takes inner strength. A student of mine, Seth, wrote a reflection about how she demonstrated empathy toward another family:

> One time I can recall being empathetic to a stranger outside of my close family and friends was during my time with the United States Air Force. My friend, Mike, had just passed away, and his family had to be notified of their son's death. Picking up that phone and dialing that number was one of the hardest things I ever had to do. I shared the grief with Mike's family and answered the hard questions they had about the final moments of their son's life.

Seth later reflected, "The only way to be truly empathetic to another person is if you have shared a similar experience at some point in your life. Without this it is impossible to know how someone really feels."

You can discuss empathy with your students and how they might act in certain situations. Empathy can be developed at any point in life, and even adults have the ability to grow further into caring and compassionate people. If someone has ever been kind to you, it's easier to pass this kindness onto someone else. But if you have never experienced empathy, it's difficult to show concern toward another person. Seth reflected on a moment when he was alone at an airport on Thanksgiving Day:

> It was Thanksgiving and I was sitting in the airport waiting for my departure to my first base with the United States Air Force. The flight was delayed until the next morning and I did not have the funds to pay for a hotel. As I found a corner to sleep in, a family approached me and asked if I lived nearby. Once I explained my situation, they invited me to their home for Thanksgiving dinner. They let me sleep at their house and gave me a ride back to the airport to catch my flight. As it turns out, the father of this family had recently retired from the army.

This act of kindness transformed Seth's life forever, making him a kinder and more compassionate person. In the best of all possible worlds, your students will both practice empathy and experience empathy from others.

MAKING AN EARLY IMPACT

How can a young person make an impact on the world? Children impact the world by giving back to society. There are so many wonderful examples, but I'll highlight just a few here:

- Malala Yousafzai is an activist for educating women in Pakistan. She was shot in the head as a young teen but subsequently recovered and went on to win the Nobel Peace Prize at age 17 for her work in human rights. Malala is currently pursuing a bachelor's degree at Oxford University.

- Greta Thurnberg is a young woman whose protests outside the Swedish Parliament snowballed into an international movement for students. At 16 years old, she was recently nominated for the Nobel Peace Prize and continues to inspire activists around the world.

- Alexandra Scott suffered from a rare form of cancer and began a fundraiser in her front yard by selling lemonade. She raised more than $1 million for cancer research before she died at the age of 8 in 2004. Many kids have started a lemonade stand to raise spending money, but very few turn an idea into a national organization. Alexandra Scott's story may inspire your students to start their own charitable projects.

When you look at your local community, you may not see luminaries like Malala, Greta, and other famous activists. But kids are making an impact through volunteering with Special Olympics, working at soup kitchens, and gathering cans for Open Pantry. Children are working behind the scenes in every community and doing remarkable things. Why shouldn't your students be part of this exciting movement?

Start where your students are, and take little steps that will translate into a big impact at your school. In *The Tipping Point: How*

Little Things Can Make a Big Difference, Gladwell (2002) stated, "Ideas and products and messages spread just like viruses do" (p. 7). There's no reason that empathy can't go viral in your classroom and school because "social epidemics are also driven by the efforts of a handful of people" (p. 11). When you spread empathy, children will understand its importance and work behind the scenes to make it into a movement. But how do you go from an idea to a teaching moment? How can you make this concept come alive in your classroom?

> **For an empathy initiative to be successful, it must be student-driven and teacher-supported.**

Show students how to think from another person's perspective. One way to do this is by leading a class discussion about something in the news. For instance, you might lead a class discussion about Greta Thurnberg's work, beginning with the following statement:

> At just 15 years old, Greta Thurnberg began protesting climate change by standing outside the Swedish Parliament. Her passion led to an international movement. What are some things we can do today to make the world a better place? Can we recycle? Can we save energy by turning off lights when we leave rooms? Let's create an action list of things we can do to make the world a better place for everyone to live in.

In response to this prompt, students can develop a list of actions they can take to make the world a better place starting today. Every time you act with empathy, you're leading students toward becoming caring and compassionate people. Every step you take is a step in the right direction.

LEADERS AND INFLUENCERS

Don't forget that many students think about empathy and implement it in their daily lives already. Some students have more knowledge than you might expect at young ages. In response to a writing prompt about the difficulties of expressing empathy, Brendan wrote:

> Expressing empathy toward someone I might not like is hard. However, I have three ways to show empathy. First, I try to be a civil human being with everyone I meet. Two, I have learned [that] forgiveness allows me to feel empathy toward those I may not like. Three, I can offer help and assistance to someone when they need it, and be nonjudgmental. If I follow these three steps, I will feel empathy toward most people.

If students experience empathy, they will understand it. But a true understanding of empathy requires life experience, too.

Within the school hierarchy, some students are influencers or leaders among their peers. These students' support is crucial for empathy to take hold in your school. For an empathy initiative to be successful, it must be student-driven and teacher-supported. Empathy is like a tide coming in. Once the water rushes in, the rising tide will carry this ideal through an entire school. If students, teachers, parents, and administrators believe in this concept, it will become the norm on your campus. When these kids stand up and make empathy a movement, wonderful new programs and actions will happen at your school and beyond.

We see this student-led activism everywhere. From the Tiananmen Square protests in 1989 to the Black Lives Matter movement of 2013, young people have been activists throughout history—changing the world through their actions and words. More recently, young people protested against the Keystone XL pipeline, and high school students led the March for Our Lives movement in Washington, DC, in 2018.

HELPING STUDENTS SET MANAGEABLE GOALS

Students are the future of the world, and everything they do matters. Every day children have original thoughts and feelings; they speak sentences that have never been said before. Children help each other behind the scenes in ways you may not be aware of. You are never too young or too old to make a positive impact on the world, and you don't have to start on a large stage.

Many young adults take a personal interest in a cause and create a business that allows them to donate part of their proceeds to charitable causes. Children have started lemonade stands and raised thousands of dollars for charity. Young people give their time and resources to the Special Olympics. Everywhere you look, children and teenagers are making a difference in the world through volunteer activities.

Although your students may begin with exciting ideas, they need a plan to be successful. Here's the good news: In the Internet age, you don't need a lot of capital to get started, just enthusiasm. But you *do* need a game plan to get from point A to point B. If you don't have a plan, you won't be successful.

Your students can develop a vision of their future community service project. What steps must they take this week to put their plan into action? Begin with a small project that can be done in a short period of time before progressing to a larger stage. Why should you start small, instead of thinking big from the start? When students achieve success at small tasks, they prepare for success on a larger stage. Think about runners; it makes sense to start with a 5K before you move to a marathon. Think about writers; you wouldn't sit down to write a 600-page novel if you've never written anything before. Start with a small goal before progressing to a larger project.

Before your students spread empathy, start with a goal that can be accomplished in weeks rather than years. Set a goal that is attainable, and students will build confidence. If your students begin with a small project, they can always build it into a larger one over time. One idea is to start a schoolwide initiative for developing empathy. You can host a focus group and collect ideas about how this project would work. You may want to start a conversation with a prompt:

> We are considering starting an empathy-related outreach program. Ideally this program will serve the entire school. Can you think of a title and mission statement for this program?

Students can brainstorm ideas about the program before they implement it. When students submit ideas, they become stakeholders in empathy. As the advisor of this project, you can guide students toward making good choices, but ultimately you'll watch their success from the sidelines. As the project takes off, your students will spread it throughout the school.

After students develop a mission statement, you can have them develop a written plan for their project. For instance, students may establish an outreach program in which new students are welcomed to school by students already attending school. This project could be like a Welcome Wagon that operates in some towns, and students could be introduced to a new school under the guidance of a "Big Brother" or "Big Sister" who knows the campus and people. When I was a student at The MacDuffie School in Springfield, MA, a "Big Sister" invited me into the community with a handwritten letter and a warm welcome when I arrived at the school. Thirty years later, I am still friends with Lisa. There's no reason why this initiative can't have the same success at your school.

START LOCAL, ACT GLOBALLY

Every time your students walk into your classroom, they have the potential to change the world. Many students don't realize the value of a single kind word or action. Some of the greatest initiatives began in school settings. In 1990, Wendy Kopp, a Princeton graduate, used her senior thesis to launch Teach for America. Today Kopp is bringing her teaching corps around the world with a new program, Teach for All. Wendy Kopp is a wonderful example of a student taking an initiative and making a national impact. What if she had put her thesis on a shelf and forgotten about it? Would the world be a different place without Teach for America?

Here's the real question: Why can't there be more Wendy Kopps? Why can't we take her spirit of philanthropy and develop it in our students? Many students don't believe they can make an impact on the world. Think about the students at Marjory Stoneman Douglas High School. They only stepped into the national spotlight after a tragic shooting happened at their school. We can't blame students for not realizing the power of a single action.

Textbooks often focus on the movers and shakers of a generation without mentioning the people who supported these movements. When we think about big impacts, the legendary astronaut Neil Armstrong comes to mind. As he stepped onto the moon, Armstrong said, "That's one small step for man, one giant leap for mankind." But Neil Armstrong was only able to accomplish his mission through the hard work of scientists, engineers, mission control, and all of the other people working at NASA. When Armstrong stepped on the moon, he represented thousands of talented people who worked at the space agency in 1969. His achievement was the result of years of research, thoughtful planning, and skilled engineering, all of which culminated in the Apollo 11 mission's success. Most of us will never walk on the moon, but every day we can make a positive difference in the world.

> **Every time your students walk into your classroom, they have the potential to change the world.**

Everything we do matters. All it takes is one caring action to make a difference. In 1983, Samantha Smith, a schoolgirl in Maine, wrote a letter to Yuri Andropov, General Secretary of the Communist Party of the Soviet Union. Here is her letter (Samantha Smith Foundation, n.d.):

> Dear Mr. Andropov,
>
> My name is Samantha Smith, and I am ten years old. Congratulations on your new job. I have been worrying about Russia and the United States getting into a nuclear war. Are you going to vote to have a war or not? If you aren't, please tell me how you are going to help to not have a war. This question you do not have to answer, but I would like to know why you want to conquer the world or at least our country. God made the world for us to live together in peace and not to fight.
>
> Sincerely,
>
> Samantha Smith

In her letter, Samantha expressed fear that the United States and Russia would end up in a nuclear war. In response, Samantha and her parents were invited to tour the Soviet Union, and their visit resulted in international press coverage. One girl's letter made a big impact on the world, demonstrating the importance of social activism at all ages.

Your students can become activists, too, sharing empathy with the world. There are many ways you can implement empathy that will complement your curriculum. For instance, if you want to develop students' writing skills, have them create greeting cards for people who live at a local nursing home. Students will develop writing and design skills while creating unique cards.

Your students can also make a difference in the way they treat each other. Saying hello to the "new girl" in school could be the first step toward a future friendship. Inviting a boy to play kickball at recess could be the first step toward a sports connection. These actions don't take a huge amount of effort, but they can make a difference on a school campus. Every time your students reach out to someone, they have the potential to make a new friend.

Empathy takes place at the individual level, but it has a positive influence on the entire group. If you wish to be proactive, assign the following writing exercise to your students:

> What can you do to become more empathetic? How can you be a positive change agent within our school?

A student, Ethan, responded to this writing prompt with the following statement:

> I don't believe there's anything I can do to make the school more empathetic. I can only control myself. Change comes at the individual level. Therefore, individuals in the classroom can become empathetic one at a time, and change the attitude of the entire class. Each student can take a step toward transforming the classroom into a place filled with empathy.

Writing about empathy makes student more aware of their feelings. First Ethan considered empathy from the viewpoint of the larger group, before contemplating what he could personally do to promote this concept. He realized that individuals working together could create a more empathetic classroom and world.

PURSUING EXCELLENCE IN EMPATHY

When students walk into your classroom, they bring their hopes, fears, and dreams. They also bring their enthusiasm, excitement, and energy. Your class has huge potential, especially at the beginning of the year. Can you utilize this energy to create a dynamic atmosphere, or will it all go to waste? Can we pursue empathy with excellence, just like history, English, and other subjects?

The best way to measure empathy is in a concerted effort that results in long-term change. Whether this effort is making friends at school or working on a volunteer project, there's always room for empathy in a school setting. Some students will achieve a moderate level of success in a volunteer project before moving onto something else. Other children will achieve great things in a project and turn it into something bigger than they ever expected.

Students can make a huge impact on smaller stages as well. Some students volunteer or coordinate a "giving tree" for needy youngsters during the holiday season. These projects are short-term but make a huge impact on people's lives. If a student signs up for a volunteer project just to put it on his resume, he will make a minimal impact. But if a child starts a project with the intent on giving back to society, she can make a huge impact in a short period of time.

FINAL THOUGHTS

A wonderful example of making an impact is the film *Mr. Holland's Opus* (Field, Cort, Nolin, Duncan, & Herek, 1995). Mr. Holland spends years creating a symphony that may never come to fruition. At the end of this movie, former students return to campus to share their appreciation with their teacher. They have succeeded in different ventures, and they all feel gratitude toward Mr. Holland. As Gertrude Lang tells Mr. Holland,

> Look around you. There is not a life in this room that you have not touched, and each of us is a better person because of you. We are your symphony, Mr. Holland. We are the melodies and the notes of your opus. We are the music of your life.

Never forget that you aren't just creating syllabi, designing curriculum, or writing points on a blackboard. You are helping children become their best selves and sharing your inspiration with the world.

DISCUSSION QUESTIONS

For Teachers

1. Look around your classroom. What small (local) actions could your students take that might result in larger (global) impacts?
2. What thought leaders do you admire? How do these people use empathy to connect and make change?
3. What kinds of activities can you plan that might spark your students' interest in becoming change agents?

For Students

1. What is a small action you can take this week to create a more empathetic classroom? How might that small action create a larger impact?
2. Young people can create change in the world. Write about someone your age who has shown leadership through empathy. What can you learn from this person?

Chapter 7

How Can You Use Technology to Promote Empathy?

Many teachers feel frustrated when children text and use their cell phones constantly. How can we get them to pay attention if they are immersed in technology? Can children learn to be critical thinkers by texting and e-mailing?

Realistically, our students are not going to give up technology anytime soon. Children born in this millennium have grown up in a world with cell phones, e-mail, and other technology at their fingertips. Whether they are working on presentations, texting their friends, posting on Instagram, or shopping online, our students are always using technology. They don't know what it's like to live in a world without cell phones or Snapchat. That's why we need to work with technology, not against it. Technology is here to stay, and it will become even more important to our students in the future. Instead of being frustrated, we may be able to use technology to help our students develop empathy.

TECHNOLOGY AS AN ASSET, NOT A LIABILITY

In the world of finance, there are assets and liabilities. In *Rich Dad Poor Dad: What the Rich Teach Their Kids About Money That the Poor and Middle Class Do Not!*, Kiyosaki and Lechter (1997) delineated the difference between assets and liabilities. Assets bring in income and increase in value over time, while liabilities cost money to maintain and depreciate in value. It may seem like a stretch to use this financial term to describe technology in our classroom, but bear with me a moment.

When we see technology as an asset within our classroom, we develop ideas for how to utilize the resources at hand to help our students become caring people. With the right mindset, technology is an asset. When we see technology as a liability, it becomes a drawback within our classroom. Therefore, our perspective on technology defines how our students see it, and their perspective impacts everything.

You teach in a classroom without walls. You make a global impact while sitting at your desk. What could be more exciting?

How do you feel about your students and technology? When you see technology as a necessity, it becomes an asset. You imagine the amazing things that technology can teach your students and all of the things that you can do with computers, cell phones, and the like. You see the possibilities of using devices for research projects.

When you see technology in your classroom through a positive lens, so many worlds of possibilities open up to you. The cell phone is a way to text a student a homework assignment, and e-mail is a wonderful way to connect with parents. The computers and devices in the classroom are a research launching point for major projects.

Technology can be a wonderful asset to serving your students in the classroom, and it provides many opportunities for teaching empathy.

USING TECHNOLOGY TO CARE

With technology at your fingertips, you have myriad resources to use with your students that were never available to previous generations of educators. You teach in a classroom without walls. You make a global impact while sitting at your desk. What could be more exciting?

You can use technology to teach your students mathematics, literacy, and empathy all at once. Students can collaborate on writing books and publishing them. Children can set up GoFundMe pages to race funds for charities. Kids can e-mail poetry to each other or collaborate on documents, turning a computer into a virtual writing workshop. The possibilities are endless, and students are probably already using these resources. Can you steer your students in a positive direction, so that they use these resources to broaden their academic and social horizons?

When I asked my students to respond to the prompt, "How can we use technology to become caring people?", Claire wrote this response:

> I love to use e-mail to work on writing projects with friends. We send poems back and forth while we are in the middle of writing them, and we edit and comment on each other's work. Technology allows us to help each other become better writers on the spot.

Claire and her friends utilized technology to conduct writing workshops. They edited each other's poetry during recess. Technology was a positive impact on their lives and writing development.

THE CELL PHONE IN THE ROOM

In the Internet age, students are more connected than ever before via social media. Today's students have grown up with technology at their fingertips. They have virtual friendships with people all over the world. But many students cannot carry on a conversation in real life. Other students may discover that a Facebook friend isn't the same as a real friend.

Can a cell phone be a drawback? In the article "Have Smartphones Destroyed a Generation?", Twenge (2017) looked at the life of a 13-year-old girl who spent the majority of her summer in her bedroom, texting friends and sending photos through Snapchat. Twenge also analyzed general trends about children born between 1995 and 2012 (who grew up with smartphones, e-mail, and Instagram accounts), finding a lack of connection, difficulty with social relations, and even depression in this age group. Your students may be more comfortable using social media than having face-to-face conversations. But they still need empathy in their lives, perhaps even more than you did at their age.

Let's think back to your childhood. Even if you are a millennial, you didn't always have access to technology day and night. You played real games in real time. Today you're working with a different audience than the children you attended school with. Along with increased exposure to and comfort with technology, your students come from more diverse backgrounds than ever before. They bring new and dynamic perspectives.

LAUNCHING EMPATHY

Take an informal survey of your classroom. What kinds of technology do your students use? Chances are they have cell phones and computers at home, and they are adept at everything from creating websites to texting friends. Your students have lived for years online. Why not ask your students to be the experts? Have your students reflect on how technology can promote empathy. Here is a starting point that you can use to launch a class discussion:

> How many people have cell phones? How can you use your cell phone to create a more caring world . . . to promote empathy? Let's get together in small groups and brainstorm ideas!

Figure 9 shares some responses that students brainstormed during a class discussion.

This list is just a starting point, and it shows how students use their phones to maintain friendships. When we see technology as a tool for creating empathy, it becomes a positive force in and outside our classrooms.

What about computers? Whether your students are working on group projects together or starting charity drives, the computer is a launching point for creativity and empathy. But the important thing to remember is that you can't rely on special effects. A multimedia presentation has to stand alone on its own quality; the graphics and special effects can't compensate for the material it contains. Although a computer allows students to collaborate on a book, they still need to proofread and write their content carefully. Remember that the computer is a great tool, but that student initiative is the driving force behind the success of every project.

HOW CAN TECHNOLOGY PROMOTE EMPATHY?

Texting friends homework assignments.

E-mailing a birthday card to a friend.

Calling friends to invite them to a party.

Taking photos with my cell phone.

Creating a photo album from my birthday party.

Keeping in touch with my parents.

Staying in touch with friends from my old town.

Figure 9. Student responses for promoting empathy through technology.

SETTING GOALS

How can you keep empathy going and growing in students' daily interactions with technology? How can you be sure that students are texting about valid issues, rather than just out of boredom? How can you know that the computer is being used as a resource, not as entertainment, within your classroom?

> **Technology is the key to connecting parents and students to your class.**

Many teachers provide students with checklists for what they must accomplish within a class session. When students are being graded on a checklist, they stick to a task. They maintain interest in a project, rather than being distracted by the Internet. They write the next section of their essay instead of texting friends. They will set up the GoFundMe page that afternoon, or come up with a strategy for doing one soon on their own time. It's up to you to set reasonable goals and to make sure your students continue to utilize technology for productive means.

TURNING TECHNOLOGY INTO A POSITIVE FORCE

As technology is here to stay, you must turn it into a positive force within your class. Technology allows you to set up a website that parents can follow, send e-mails to your class, and keep track of students' grades electronically. You can text a parent with important information or turn your classroom knowledge into a PowerPoint presentation. The entire world is literally at your fingertips!

Technology is a powerful force in classrooms today, even if it is sometimes intrusive. Teachers who work in classrooms filled with computers sometimes wish they could teach with less technology, while other teachers flourish with minimal resources. When you turn this technology into a positive force, you transform cell phones into resources and computers into areas of the classroom where students can develop projects. You invest your time and effort in teaching, yet it's nice to know that you can post your lessons online so students who are absent can make up the work. Best of all, it's nice when you can text or e-mail parents in emergency situations. Sometimes you may wonder how you survived in a pretechnology era where people didn't carry cell phones or have access to computers. You'll find that these tools are valuable for developing empathy in and outside your classroom, and that technology is the key to connecting parents and students to your class.

Technology allows you to make your classroom a global place. One day your students will work with colleagues from around the world in a company or workplace without walls. Why not start developing critical communication skills today?

JOBS OF THE FUTURE WILL REQUIRE EMPATHY

What kind of career will your students have? When we think about future careers, it's difficult to anticipate what kids could end up doing. Figure 10 lists some of the careers that will continue into the future, even if their skill sets evolve. What is the common thread that links all of these careers together? Empathy! This list is a starting point, and you can add items to the list as you think of them.

Whether you are teaching or working as a parole officer, it's critical to feel empathy for the people you work with. When your students enter the workforce, they will deal with people from all walks of life. If you work in sales or marketing, you must understand the needs of your customers. There's no substitute for seeing things from your client's perspective or understanding what your customer wants. You can know a great deal about diseases and pathogens, but you'll be far more successful as a doctor or scientist if you understand people as well. It's never too early to appreciate a diversity of cultures, opinions, and backgrounds. Empathy is critical in every field.

- Doctor
- Lawyer
- Public relations manager
- Financial advisor
- Advertising sales agent
- Teacher
- Salesperson
- Television reporter
- Counselor
- Builder
- Coach
- Writer/blogger
- Engineer
- Nurse
- Artist
- Scientist
- Professor
- Website designer
- Publisher
- Veteran
- Firefighter
- Police officer
- Editor
- Judge

Figure 10. Careers that involve empathy.

FINAL THOUGHTS

Technology may be the key to a classroom filled with empathy. After all, we use cell phones, e-mail, and other technology to touch base with students outside of our classrooms and to mentor children beyond school walls. Technology allows students to connect in both formal and informal ways—from taking pictures of each other to developing projects together. The wonderful thing about technology is that it allows students and teachers to express empathy much more spontaneously than years ago. When we use technology wisely, our students will begin to see that technology can build bridges within our classroom and across the entire world.

DISCUSSION QUESTIONS

For Teachers

1. How can you think of technology as an asset rather than a liability?
2. What strategies work best for bringing technology into your classroom?
3. Can you think of some more positive ways to integrate technology and empathy?

For Students

1. How can you use technological devices, like cell phones and computers, to develop a caring classroom and school?
2. What do you like best about technology? Does it allow you to develop deeper friendships or connect with people who move away?
3. What are some pros and cons of using technology to communicate with others?

Chapter 8

How Can You Lead a Schoolwide Empathy Initiative?

> The greatest gift of human beings is that we have the power of empathy.
>
> —Meryl Streep

When you became a teacher, you also became a leader. What you do matters. Every word you speak and every action you take are consequential. Think about the teachers who inspired you to become the best student you could be. Why do these people stand out? Did they care about you outside their classroom? If you can replicate these methods in your classroom, you can make a difference, too.

How can you lead empathy in your school? Start in your own classroom. Students are accustomed to antibullying campaigns, which focus on preventing cruel behavior toward students. However, these programs fail to look at the root cause of bullying: a lack of concern for the well-being of other people. You can address this root cause by teaching your students how to think from different perspectives. Starting with a small step can change the atmosphere of an entire school. As Marian Wright Edelman once said, "You really can change the world if you care enough."

Consider sharing "The Starfish Story" by Loren Eisley (as cited in Edib, 2009) with your students. This story teaches how one person can make a huge difference in the world through a single action:

> One day a man was walking along the beach when he noticed a boy picking something up and gently throwing it into the ocean. Approaching the boy, he asked, "What are you doing?" The youth replied, "Throwing starfish back into the ocean. The surf is up and the tide is going out. If I don't throw them back, they'll die." "Son," the man said, "don't you realize there are miles and miles of beach and hundreds of starfish? You can't make a difference! After listening politely, the boy bent down, picked up another starfish, and threw it back into the surf. Then, smiling at the man, he said, "I made a difference for that one." (para. 1)

When students hear this story, they will realize that every action they take can make a positive impact on the world. How can you turn this story into a teaching moment? Here is a prompt that I created around this classic story:

> Think of a small action that you can take to make a difference in the world. Whether you are picking up a piece of litter, dropping off cookies at a nursing home, or helping a friend finish homework, figure out what you are going to do. Now, write a short story in which you explain to a bystander why this action makes a difference in the world. You may use "The Starfish Story" as a starting point for your own story.

You'll be surprised at the stories that students write about making an impact on the world. Through small actions, you can make a huge difference in another person's life—and the story format allows students to examine these positive impacts in detail.

WORKING WITH YOUR COLLEAGUES

Empathy can take a lifetime to learn, but the best place to start is with the people you know. Many teachers want to work in a kinder and gentler environment. With your colleagues, discuss empathy and how to bring it into your classroom in holistic ways. Other teachers may already be implementing empathy in their own classrooms and have great ideas for how to spread it through your school.

When colleagues inquire, provide resources and suggestions for how to implement empathy in their classes. Network with fellow instructors to promote empathy in a way that reflects your school's mission statement. The more people you get involved, the more likely you will achieve success.

Some teachers believe that initiatives take away time from required activities. But if you can get other faculty on board, empathy will spread more quickly than if it's just implemented in your classroom. With the support of your principal, you can create a schoolwide movement to promote empathy. Consider giving the program a catchy name to spark interest, such as "Every Voice Matters" or "Toward a Caring School."

Empathy can take a lifetime to learn, but the best place to start is with the people you know.

As you create a schoolwide initiative, also solicit ideas from students. Students are the power behind these ideas, and they will determine whether the initiative flourishes or dies. When seeking student ideas, keep an open mind. Start with the following question as a journal entry:

> You are asked to help set up a special program that will encourage students to be more empathetic. Come up with a name for this program and a plan for how it will be implemented across the school.

When I assigned this question on a test, I received many responses ranging from a student outreach program that would allow students to connect across the school, to a "Become a Better Leader Plan" that would provide children with special events and activities geared at developing leadership skills.

One student, Lisa, developed the idea for a documentary that would help students develop empathy, titled "Walking a Mile in Their Shoes":

> This program will consist of short films played in schools. These films will include separate clips of students going through the same thing, but they're expressing how they feel alone. Later on in the film, they all come together and share their feelings and come to a better understanding of each other.

Another student, Samantha, developed the idea for an anonymous outreach program titled "Reach." She stated:

> This program will be implemented across high schools in America. It's for students who are afraid to talk to a guidance counselor or parent about things. Students volunteer anonymously, sending

and receiving letters from each other. They can talk about their mental health struggles or anything at all, and send it to another volunteer. These people give advice and empathetic feedback in their responses, and nobody has to know who the writers are.

Another student, Ethan, believed that empathy was best taught in the classroom. He stated,

The name of this program will be "Empathy 101," and it will be a required course that teaches students how to respect others and their feelings. The program will go into the external and internal ways to show empathy and will greatly improve life around campus.

In all of these cases, students simply brainstormed these ideas; it would be interesting to see these ideas developed into full-fledged initiatives. If students can conceptualize program names and tenets in just a few minutes, what could do they do during the course of a semester? What could they accomplish during an entire school year?

STARTING YOUR EMPATHY INITIATIVE

When empathy flourishes, it becomes a natural part of the school culture. Students text and check up on each other before exams. Faculty meet in groups to discuss how to improve their teaching plans. Everywhere you look, you'll see empathy growing in students, staff, faculty, and even parents. In a 21st-century world, empathy flourishes in the classroom and in cyberspace long after the school day is finished through texts, e-mails, and other technological means.

The truth is, you need concrete ideas to begin your initiative (not warm, fuzzy thoughts). Whether you are helping students begin a new community service project or supervising a play in which your entire class contributes, you'll discover that an enormous amount of work is involved in turning a dream into a reality. But the results can be amazing. Students have developed friendships with pen pals around the world. Kids have turned their volunteer projects into businesses. Children have reached out to friends in need. When empathy flourishes, it spreads to the entire school. Suddenly it becomes a "cool" thing to do.

Can an entire campus feel empathy? A student, Lani, wrote about her experiences moving and transferring schools:

> I experienced empathy when I transferred to Florida Gulf Coast University. When I applied to FGCU, I was coming from Puerto Rico because of Hurricane Maria. My transcripts did not arrive on time. They [the school personnel] helped me with scholarships and waited patiently for the documents. The school even sponsored an activity to welcome students transferring from universities there. They cared for us and we all felt welcome.

Lani's statement shows that empathy can grow across a campus until it becomes a welcoming place for everyone.

In a 21st-century world, empathy flourishes in the classroom and in cyberspace long after the school day is finished.

ESTABLISHING A SCHOOL INITIATIVE THROUGH READING

How can we help students connect with each other? In a school setting, students are divided by age and ability level. It's difficult for students to relate to each other if they have never had a class or extracurricular activity together, especially if they are in different grade levels.

Can students find common ground when they don't know each other? On many college campuses, first-year students read and study a book together. This idea may not work in a setting where children's ages range from 5–12, but there are other ways to create connections.

Many schools host a yearly "Invited Author" day in which a notable writer is invited to campus to give presentations. Principals invite an author whose books appeal to children of many ages. Reading a book together can be a great activity to kick-start an empathy movement at your school, and it's a great way to prepare students to be more engaged when an author visits their classroom.

The division of children by grade and age is arbitrary. Many students go through the entire school system without socializing with anyone 12 months older or younger than themselves. Eventually they graduate into a world where people of all ages and backgrounds work together. The arbitrary divisions created in schools work against students when they have to go out into the "real world" and network with people across different backgrounds.

With a school reading initiative, students will read the same story or learn about the same author. They will have a common intellectual and emotional experience. You can lead students toward finding common connections while reading the same book at the same time. But the most important voices of empathy are your students'. Students need a voice in creating a caring culture.

HELP STUDENTS CONNECT WITH EACH OTHER

How can students connect with each other? In a school setting, boundaries are built through classes, sports, and in the cafeteria. With encouragement from you, students will mingle with peers they've never spoken with before. When students meet new people, they'll discover the limitations of eating lunch with the same group every day. They will stretch outside their comfort zones and meet new friends.

Marina Keegan (2015) wrote a poignant essay, "The Opposite of Loneliness," shortly before graduating from Yale. In this essay, Keegan described the web of friends she found at her university and the multiple ways that students connected with each other:

> We don't have a word for the opposite of loneliness, but if we did, I could say that's what I want in life. What I'm grateful and thankful to have found at Yale, and what I'm scared of losing when we wake up tomorrow and leave this place (p. 1)

Although Keegan was lucky enough to have a web of friendships, not every student finds a circle of friends within an academic setting. Some students are left out of cliques and not invited to parties.

You cannot force friendships, but you *can* watch children develop new and exciting connections.

At the beginning of the year, students meet new people and form dynamic friendships. But as the year progresses, it's easy to fall into a comfort zone in which students only work with their friends on group projects. What can we do to keep our students forming new friendships and meeting new people? As the year continues, it's helpful to continue general dialogues. I asked students to respond to the following prompt:

> As the year progresses, it's easy to fall into old patterns. What can we do to meet new people? What are some ideas that we can engage in later in the year?

In response, Casey noted,

> One way we can improve is by holding special events where people can relate to others and share their feelings in a controlled and nonjudgmental environment. The way we could make the classroom more empathetic is by having a class or two a month where we all open up and talk about something that is bothering us and get advice from our peers. This could be very helpful for many students.

By keeping lines of dialogue open, students will continue to meet new people and break down barriers that exist between cliques. When students meet new people, they'll develop a wider circle of friends.

What can you do to make this happen? You can randomly place students in groups together and assign projects that require students to network with their new group. This process encourages students to work with peers they do not know. Not only does it promote friendship, but it also encourages empathy. Every time your students stretch beyond their social confines and meet new people, they'll develop concern for others. You cannot force friendships, but you *can* watch children develop new and exciting connections.

Your students will have wonderful ideas for how to meet new people and promote empathy as the year progresses. Why not ask them? When students think about these issues, they become more conscious of the need to reach out to new people—even if these people are outside their circle of friends.

FINAL THOUGHTS

In order to create a caring school, you must get people involved. Make parents and students stakeholders in this process. The value of the initiative will be determined not only by the leadership, but also by the participants.

When your students internalize empathy, they are taking the first step toward creating a caring school. Perhaps the greatest metaphor for creating a caring school is demonstrated in the classic film *The Wizard of Oz* (LeRoy & Fleming, 1939). In this narrative, Dorothy, the Scarecrow, the Lion, and the Tin Man set off to find the Wizard of Oz. They travel down a yellow brick road, encountering obstacles and difficulties along the way. When the travelers reach the wizard, he gives tokens that represent what the travelers are looking for. The internal qualities they seek—a heart, a brain, courage, and the ability to return home—they must find within themselves.

Every year, your students begin a heroic and imaginative quest in your classroom. You can lead them toward empathy, but the end result—a caring school—is determined by each individual's dedication to empathy. Students will determine whether they attend school in a kind, gentle environment or not. But here's the most exciting thing: You can support their journey every step of the way.

DISCUSSION QUESTIONS

For Teachers

1. How can you encourage other teachers to become stakeholders in a caring school?
2. What challenges might you experience when trying to implement a schoolwide empathy program? How can you overcome these challenges?
3. What teachers in your school do you admire? How are they using empathy in their daily work?

For Students

1. You've experienced and shown empathy in class. Now it's time to take this concept to the rest of the school! How can you demonstrate empathy toward students you don't know?
2. What can you do to feel more connected to other students in your school? Besides attending class and participating in extracurricular activities, how can you meet other students?

What Is Your Future Vision of Empathy?

> Wherever there is a human being, there is an opportunity for a kindness.
>
> —Seneca

As educators, we make an impact that lasts for generations. Our influence stretches beyond our classrooms and into the world. Whatever we do to promote empathy will reap dividends many years into the future.

But making a difference in the world takes work and planning. We aren't just teaching content; we're witnessing life-transforming moments in our classroom. In *Our Town* (Wilder, 1938/2013), a character asks the famous question, "Do any human beings ever realize life while they live it—every, every minute?" (p. 108). As educators, are we appreciating every minute and every student? Are we making the most of our resources at hand to make a difference in the world?

When we look at our responsibilities, it's daunting. Many educators struggle with multiple demands on their time—from preparing students for standardized tests to dealing with behavioral issues. But our primary responsibility is preparing future citizens of the world.

Could anything be more challenging (or more rewarding)? We aren't just developing syllabi and tests; we're teaching students how to become their best selves. We must consider whether our students are receiving the attention they deserve in our classes. This isn't about grades and homework, but about treating each student as an important contributor. Every student must become indispensable within our classroom and school.

> The teacher who can read beneath the surface will connect at a higher level with her students.

We are limited by time, place, and our own life experiences. We can't see exactly where our students are coming from, but we try to understand. In *Death in the Afternoon*, Ernest Hemingway (1932/1996) developed his famous iceberg theory, in which the great mass of life is invisible and hidden beneath the surface. Hemingway wrote, "The dignity of movement of the iceberg is due to only one-eighth of it being above water. The writer who omits things because he does not know them only makes hollow places in his writing" (p. 162). As teachers, we only see our students for a few hours each day, and we only see their outward impression. Yet this iceberg reveals more than it conceals; the teacher who can read beneath the surface will connect at a higher level with her students. Although we may never develop a full understanding of our students, we can do our best to be supportive figures in their lives.

TIPPING POINTS

Gladwell's (2002) *The Tipping Point* is a wonderful analysis of how small gestures can impact the world. Gladwell drew a connection between ideas and viruses, both of which spread throughout a population quickly. When influential people use new ideas and products, the greater population takes notice.

As an educator, you are an influencer. Your ideas and actions resonate across an entire community.

Gladwell (2002) also discussed a traditional belief in advertising—that you must see or hear something six times before you remember it. In order to "stick," a message must be memorable. In the same way, people must experience empathy in their own lives before they can share it with others. Whether they witness empathy or experience it directly, an emotional connection helps this concept stick more readily than if it is taught as an abstract quality.

One way to make empathy stick is to bring it directly into a class discussion about current events. For example, in May 2019, Amanda Eller was lost in the Hawaii forest for 2 weeks when she took a jog. She was found by several volunteers who were flying by in a helicopter. More than 1,000 people searched for this woman during the 16 days that she was missing. This event is a wonderful example of empathy, but how can you use it as a launching pad for a class discussion? Here's the prompt:

> Amanda Eller was lost for 2 weeks in the rainforest. What do you think was going through her mind? How did she mentally survive this ordeal? How would you survive a situation like this?

Students can imagine what it would feel like to be lost for so many days. Then, students can discuss how they would feel in this situation. Would they feel hopeful? Would there be moments when they wanted to give up? To liven this discussion, you can share a news report about this story with students before beginning the discussion.

As an educator, you are an influencer. Your ideas and actions resonate across an entire community. You are the coach who encourages children to finish the race when they fall down midstream. You are the leader who inspires kids to learn with their hearts and not just their minds. You are revered and respected far beyond the confines of your classroom. You not only have authority, but you also have influence. You have the potential to plant empathy and to watch it grow in children's lives.

OBSTACLES

In fictional stories, characters rise to the occasion and overcome obstacles. The story arc features a character who wants something. This character encounters obstacles before either getting what he wants—or not. At the end, there is a resolution tying together loose ends in the story. As educators, we face obstacles every day. These obstacles may be external—dealing with budget issues and standardized tests. They may be internal, such as dealing with self-doubt. These obstacles also relate to our students, who may not be receptive to a class activity or attentive to a class lecture. None of us work in perfect environments, and there are obstacles to overcome during the course of a single day.

Let's talk about you. What happens when you feel overwhelmed? How do you deal with adversity? When I used to compete on a cross-country team, our theme was, "The hill that doesn't kill me makes me stronger." (It wasn't until years later that I discovered we had adapted a famous Friedrich Nietzsche saying.) This theory crosses into life's mainstream when we consider all of the obstacles we undergo in life—from losing loved ones to paying taxes. Successful people deal with what life throws at them, while people who become discouraged fail. If you're dealing with adversity right now, you're in good company. Can you maintain a positive attitude and triumph over these obstacles? Or will you become so discouraged that you quit trying?

Let's face it. Teaching is a difficult profession. In "Why Do Teachers Quit," Riggs (2013) stated that 40%–50% of teachers quit within 5 years of entering the classroom. Many people who go through teacher training never enter the classroom in the first place. These numbers are disheartening, but you don't have to be a statistic. You can work hard to become the 50%–60% percent of teachers who make teaching a career.

As teachers, we're evaluated at every twist in the road. We teach to the test, even though we'd prefer to share our love of learning with students. We buy thousands of dollars of supplies on our own dime, knowing the only reimbursement we'll get are smiling students. Most of us receive very little affirmation for the good work we're doing. Each year we come back with enthusiasm to work with another group of students. We're always becoming better teachers and people.

The best part of your job isn't teaching content. It's those unexpected moments when you can connect learning with empathy.

Recall the famous poem "The Road Not Taken," and heed Robert Frost's advice about charting your own path as an educator. You must take the road less traveled, even though it seems riskier and more challenging than the path you are on. After all, you are preparing students for an unpredictable future. You must teach your students critical thinking and creativity, not just factual information. You must think outside the box and consider what students need to know in 2050, not just today. You must take risks, and one of these risks is going outside your comfort zone.

Most importantly, you must inspire your students to become better people. The film *Dead Poets Society* (Haft, Thomas, Witt, & Weir, 1989) is a wonderful example of how a teacher can electrify a group of students to pursue learning on their own. When the boys stand in front of an old trophy case, Mr. Keating asks students to follow the Latin creed "carpe diem" and to seize the day. Years after seeing this film for the first time, I'm still inspired by the scene in which Mr. Keating encourages students to read poetry with their hearts rather than seeing it as words upon the page.

As educators, we must inspire our students so that they aren't just reading words on the page but absorbing the content. We must encourage students to take intellectual risks, even if they fail to understand ideas. We must help young people encounter new ideas and meet new people.

EFFORT AND REWARD

When you set a high bar for yourself, you're bound to fail at some point. You'll feel disappointed and wonder whether your efforts are worth it. But there's nothing worse than failing to try. When you try and fail, at least you did your very best. You put yourself out there and prepared for success later down the road. Failure isn't the end of the road; it is a step toward eventual success.

We never know what impact our instruction had in the classroom. The true extent of what we teach cannot be measured. We may never find out if our students had life-changing experiences or if our lesson was just another class period for them. We cannot tell if our students had a transformative moment in our classroom. At the end of the year, it's difficult to see if we made an impact. Did we connect with every student? Did we make a difference? These questions cannot be measured through traditional means. Students leave our classrooms without letting us know how we changed their lives. But we must strive for excellence and make a difference in the world.

As educators, we teach required material and skills to our students. Our daily objectives merge into a semester that is productive and educational. We dream about going beyond the textbook and inspiring students' hopes and dreams. But we're limited to teaching a specific curriculum and to making sure our students learn factual information. Kids need to know X, Y, and Z, and there's no way around it. But the best part of your job isn't teaching content. It's those unexpected moments when you can connect learning with empathy. Never forget that you can make a difference in the world every day. You are respected and appreciated by students in ways you may never understand.

FINAL THOUGHTS

Creating a caring educational system and world is challenging, so focus on becoming the best teacher you can be and bringing all of your passion into the classroom. When you bring kindness into your life, other people will mirror this feeling back to you.

References

Association of American Colleges and Universities. (2019). *College students are more diverse than ever. Faculty and administrators are not.* Retrieved from https://www.aacu.org/aacu-news/newsletter/2019/march/facts-figures

Baron-Cohen, S., & Wheelwright, S. (2004). The empathy quotient: An investigation of adults with Asperger syndrome or high functioning autism, and normal sex differences. *Journal of Autism and Developmental Disorders, 34,* 163–175.

Beldoch, M. (1964). Sensitivity in emotional expressions in three modes of communication. In J. R. Davitz (Ed.), *The communication of emotional meaning* (pp. 31–42). New York, NY: McGraw-Hill.

Bell, K. (2009). Empathy: Not such a soft skill. *Harvard Business Review.* Retrieved from https://hbr.org/2009/05/empathy-not-such-a-soft-skill

Bloom, B. S. (Ed.). (1985). *Developing talent in young people.* New York, NY: Ballantine Books.

Campbell, J. (1993). *The hero with a thousand faces.* New York, NY: Gardner Books.

Carnegie, D. (1981). *How to win friends and influence people: The only book you need to lead you to success.* New York, NY: Pocket Books.

Chen, P. W. (2007). *Final exam: A surgeon's reflections on mortality.* New York, NY: Bantam.

Creech, S. (2011). *Walk two moons.* New York, NY: HarperCollins. (Original work published 1994)

Davis, P. (2018). We mourn George H. W. Bush, and the presidency's loss of dignity. *The Washington Post.* Retrieved from https://www.washingtonpost.com/opinions/we-mourn-george-hw-bush-and-the-presidencys-loss-of-dignity/2018/12/01/1a5f da3a-f5a0-11e8-bc79-68604ed88993_story.html

Deobald, J. (2019). Empathy is no longer a soft skill for leaders. *Forbes.* Retrieved from https://www.forbes.com/sites/forbesagen cycouncil/2019/05/14/empathy-is-no-longer-a-soft-skill-for-lead ers

Dillard, A. (2009). *An American childhood.* New York, NY: Harper-Collins.

Duckworth, A., & Gross, J. J. (2014). Self-control and grit: Related but separable determinants of success. *Current Directions in Psychological Science, 23,* 319–325.

Edib, T. (2009). *The starfish story—original story by Loren Eisley.* Retrieved from http://www.ataturksociety.org/the-starfish-sto ry-original-story-by-loren-eisley

Field, T., Cort, R. W., Nolin, M., Duncan, P. S. (Producers), & Herek, S. (Director). (1995). *Mr. Holland's opus* [Motion picture]. United States: Hollywood Pictures.

Fulghum, R. (2004). *All I ever really needed to know I learned in kindergarten: Uncommon thoughts on common things.* New York, NY: Ballantine Books.

Gardner, H. (1995). Reflections on multiple intelligences: Myths and messages. *Phi Delta Kappan, 77,* 200–209.

Gardner, H. (1999). *Intelligence reframed: Multiple intelligences for the 21st century.* New York, NY: Basic Books. (Original work published 1983)

Gardner, H. (2011). *Frames of mind: The theory of multiple intelligences*. New York, NY: Basic Books.

Gladwell, M. (2002). *The tipping point: How little things can make a big difference*. New York, NY: Little, Brown.

Gladwell, M. (2008). *Outliers: The story of success*. New York, NY: Little, Brown.

Goleman, D. (1995). *Emotional intelligence: Why it can matter more than IQ*. New York, NY: Bantam.

Goleman, D. (2006). *Social intelligence: The new science of human relationships*. New York, NY: Bantam.

Graham, S. (n.d.). Bullying: A module for teachers. *American Psychological Association*. Retrieved from https://www.apa.org/education/k12/bullying

Haft, S., Thomas, T., Witt, P. J. (Producers), & Weir, P. (Director). (1989). *Dead poets society* [Motion picture]. United States: Touchstone Pictures.

Hemingway, E. (1996). *Death in the afternoon*. New York, NY: Scribner. (Original work published 1932)

Henshon, J. (2019). On shooting free throws. *Newsletter of The Roxbury Latin School*, 9.

ITV Report. (2018). *Princess Eugenie 'an inspiration' says spinal surgeon as she shows off operation scars in Peter Pilotto dress*. Retrieved from https://www.itv.com/news/2018-10-12/princess-eugenie-speaks-out-about-showing-people-your-scars-as-she-shares-wedding-day-with-charity

Jarvis, F. W. (2000). *With love and prayers: A headmaster speaks to the next generation*. Boston, MA: Godine.

Jensen, F. E., & Nutt, A. E. (2015). *The teenage brain: A neuroscientist's survival guide to raising adolescents and young adults*. New York, NY: Harper.

Keegan, M. (2015). *The opposite of loneliness: Essays and stories*. New York, NY: Scribner.

Keller, H. (1996). *The story of my life*. New York, NY: Penguin. (Original work published 1903)

Kiyosaki, R. T., & Lechter, S. L. (1997). *Rich dad poor dad: What the rich teach their kids about money that the poor and middle class do not!* New York, NY: Warner Books.

Kopp, W. (2003). *One day all children: The unlikely triumph of Teach for America and what I learned along the way.* Cambridge, MA: Public-Affairs.

Kuhn, T. S. (2012). *The structure of scientific revolutions* (50th anniversary ed.). Chicago, IL: The University of Chicago Press. (Original work published 1962)

Lanzoni, S. (2015). A short history of empathy. *The Atlantic.* Retrieved from https://www.theatlantic.com/health/archive/2015/10/a-short-history-of-empathy/409912

Lanzoni, S. (2018). *Empathy: A history.* Grand Rapids, MI: Yale University Press.

Leonard, E. (2019). Four ways to use empathy effectively. *Psychology Today.* Retrieved from https://www.psychologytoday.com/us/blog/peaceful-parenting/201905/four-ways-use-empathy-effectively

LeRoy, M. (Producer), & Fleming, V. (Director). (1939). *The wizard of Oz.* United States: Metro-Goldwyn-Mayer.

Lindbergh, A. M. (1955). *Gift from the sea.* New York, NY: Knopf Doubleday.

The Loomis Chaffee School. (2019). *Senior Beatrice Dang publishes "Those Who Served" as Norton fellowship project.* Retrieved from https://www.loomischaffee.org/about-us/news-calendar/news-post/~post/senior-beatice-dang-20190520

Lowry, L. (1993). *The giver.* New York, NY: Houghton Mifflin Harcourt.

Maslow, A. H. (2013). *A theory of human motivation.* New York, NY: Simon & Schuster. (Original work published 1943)

Mayer, J. D., & Salovey, P. (1993). The intelligence of emotional intelligence. *Intelligence, 17,* 431–442.

McPhee, J. (1978). *A sense of where you are.* New York, NY: Farrar, Straus and Giroux.

Montgomery, L. M. (2014). *Anne of green gables*. New York, NY: Aladdin. (Original work published 1908)

Noonan, J. (2011). On this day: Anne Frank's diary published. *Finding-Dulcinea*. Retrieved from http://www.findingdulcinea.com/news/on-this-day/May-June-08/On-this-Day--Anne-Frank-s-Diary-Published-for-the-First-Time.html

Pink, D. H. (2006). *A whole new mind: Why right-brainers will rule the future*. New York, NY: Penguin.

Pink, D. H. (2009). *Drive: The surprising truth about what motivates us*. New York, NY: Riverhead Books.

Riggs, L. (2013). Why do teachers quit? *The Atlantic*. Retrieved from https://www.theatlantic.com/education/archive/2013/10/why-do-teachers-quit/280699

Samantha Smith Foundation. (n.d.). *Samantha's letter*. Retrieved from https://www.samanthasmith.info/index.php/history/letter

Seuss, Dr. (1957). *How the Grinch stole Christmas!* New York, NY: Random House.

Tennyson, A. (1842). *Ulysses*. Retrieved from https://www.poetryfoundation.org/poems/45392/ulysses

Twenge, J. M. (2017). Have smartphones destroyed a generation? *The Atlantic*. Retrieved from https://www.theatlantic.com/magazine/archive/2017/09/has-the-smartphone-destroyed-a-generation/534198

Wilder, T. (2013). *Our town: A play in three acts*. New York, NY: HarperCollins. (Original work published 1938)

About the Author

Suzanna E. Henshon, Ph.D., taught composition and creative writing for 13 years. Before receiving her Ph.D. in gifted education at William & Mary, Sue studied at the University of Chicago (M.A.) and Wesleyan University (B.A.). She has more than 400 publications, including several novels and three books with Prufrock Press, *King Arthur's Academy*, *Haunted House: Descriptive and Narrative Writing Exercises*, and *Mystery Science: The Case of the Missing Bicycle* (with Diego Patino). Her most recent book, *Write Your Book This Week!*, was published in 2019.